Imaging the
WORD

Imaging the
WORD

An Arts and Lectionary Resource

Susan A. Blain, Editor
Sharon Iverson Gouwens
Catherine O'Callaghan
Grant Spradling

Volume 2

United Church Press

Cleveland, Ohio

Thomas E. Dipko	Executive Vice President, UCBHM
Ansley Coe Throckmorton	General Secretary, Division of Education and Publication
Lynne M. Deming	Publisher
Sidney D. Fowler	Editor for Curriculum Resources
Kathleen C. Ackley	Associate Editor for Curriculum Resources
Monitta Lowe	Editorial Assistant
Marjorie Pon	Managing Editor
Kelley Baker	Editorial Assistant
Cynthia Welch	Production Manager
Martha A. Clark	Art Director
Lynn Keller	Business Manager
Paul Tuttle	Marketing Director
Angela M. Fasciana	Sales and Distribution Manager

United Church Press, Cleveland, Ohio 44115
© 1995 by United Church Press
Imaging the Word has been designed to be used with *Word Among Us: A Worship-centered, Lectionary-based Curriculum for Congregations* and with the New Revised Standard Version of the Bible. All scripture quotations, unless otherwise noted, are from the New Revised Standard Version of the Bible, © 1989 by the Division of Christian Education of the National Council of the Churches of Christ in the U.S.A. Adaptations have been made for clarity and inclusiveness. Used by permission.

Pages 266 to 277 constitute an extension of this copyright page. We have made every effort to trace copyrights on the materials included in this publication. If any copyrighted material has nevertheless been included without permission and due acknowledgment, proper credit will be inserted in future printings after receipt of notice.
All rights reserved. Published 1995

Printed in Hong Kong on acid-free paper
First printing, 1995

Design: Kapp & Associates, Inc., Cleveland, Ohio
Cover art: Paul Gauguin, *Vision after the Sermon,* detail, National Gallery of Scotland, Edinburgh, Great Britain (Bridgeman/Art Resource, N.Y.). Used by permission.
Jacopo Bassano, *The Miraculous Draught of Fishes,* detail, Matthieson Fine Arts, London, England. Used by permission.

Library of Congress Cataloging–in–Publication Data
(Revised for v. 2.)

Lawrence, Kenneth T. (Kenneth Todd), 1935–
Imaging the Word.

May be used in conjunction with "Word among us" Sunday School curriculum published by United Church Press.
Includes bibliographical references and index.

1. Church year. 2. Revised common lectionary. 3. Bible—Illustrations. 4. Bible—In literature. 5. United Church of Christ—Education. 6. United churches—United States—Education. 7. Reformed Church—United States—Education. 8. Christian education—Textbooks for adults—United Church of Christ. 9. Christian education—Textbooks for children—United Church of Christ. I. Weaver, Jan Cather, 1955– . II. Wedell, Roger William. III. Title.

BV30.L39 1994   263'.9   94–823

ISBN 0–8298–0970–8 (cloth : v. 1 : acid–free paper)
ISBN 0–8298–0971–6 (pbk. : v. 1 : acid–free paper)
ISBN 0–8298–1032–3 (cloth : v. 2 : acid–free paper)
ISBN 0–8298–1033–1 (pbk. : v. 2 : acid–free paper)

Note: The editor and writers for volume 2 are Susan A. Blain, Sharon Iverson Gouwens, Catherine O'Callaghan, and Grant Spradling.

Contents

Foreword

Manuel Alvarez Bravo, *The Public Fountain*

Drawn from our daily lives and shaped by what we are confronted with, our religious identity is formed by our experiences—whether or not we are aware of it. We may become what we watch, buy, desire, and think. What we do, pray, and imagine shapes us. We are what we give ourselves to. Images—whether found on a television, movie, or computer screen; in magazines or newspapers; at home, worship, or play; of what we eat, drink, wear, read, or listen to—play a particular role in such formation. *Imaging the Word* invites you to take in selected Bible passages and images and writings from the arts.

The passages from the Bible included in *Imaging the Word* were selected from the *Revised Common Lectionary*, which is a listing of Bible readings for congregational life, worship, and preaching to be used throughout the church year. For each week and selected festivals, the readings often include passages from the Hebrew Scriptures, including the Psalms, and a portion of a Gospel and one other Christian scripture. In this volume, one reading is selected as the focus for each unit. Because *Imaging the Word* is coordinated with the educational component of *Word Among Us* that begins in September, this volume begins with the readings for Proper 17 (the thirteenth Sunday following the festival of Pentecost).

Visual images, writings, and commentary were not simply selected to illustrate a passage, although some of the arts are representational. Rather, selections were made to invite you to discover God through the Bible reading, to provide artistic symbols of the passage for your memory, to connect the passage with your life, and to look for God's Word in the world around you. The selections are choices that may delight you, baffle you, offend you, or lead you to prayer and action. By viewing, considering, and questioning these choices, perhaps you will be able to recall or imagine images and text that you would have included.

In order to foster identity, view *Imaging the Word* with your imagination. To read the Bible in faith requires prayerful imagination to join God's Hebrew and Christian people—to enter their unique ancient world. Your imagination will take you to biblical places and times. While considering the passages, the art selections will also send you to other places and times. Even the colors, shapes, sounds, and words may touch emotions as well as thought. Imagination involves a voluntary displacement from one's own limitations of experience; you may discover something new or may be open to what was hidden before. Even after viewing the most abstract of paintings, John Gilmour says "it highlights features of the world we tend to overlook by isolating our attention on such factors as color relationships. . . . After intense involvement with art works we return to the world with new eyes." Through imaginative engagement, drawing on Scripture and the arts, we may be transformed.

Along with being people of imagination, you and your community are invited to be interpreters. The more one looks into the Bible, the better one may be able to interpret the arts and the world around him or her. The more one interprets the gifts of art, the more one will be able to uncover the Word among the words of the Bible.

Interpreting is more than answering "What does this mean?" Rather it explores the question "What does this disclose or reveal?" An answer to that question may include a statement of belief, but will demand more. It requires spirituality, imagination, feeling, choices, and action. To explore the question of disclosure or revelation, draw upon many sources. Prayer and contemplation are basic to interpreting for people of faith. The revelation of God and God's way is what one seeks. Also draw upon your own thoughts, feelings, and experiences as well as those of your community. Discover the world of the writers and artists, and the world that surrounds the artist, the writer, and you.

Interpretation offers the opportunity for you to make choices—not to passively view an image or text. Drawing upon sources that describe social and historical context or that help you learn to interpret, you will be better able to identify the truth or power revealed in a particular text or object of art. You will then decide how to follow up those moments of interpretation. Does this reading compel you to forgive? Does this photo impel you to act? Does this music move you to love? Can you honestly pray this prayer? You, who have drawn in image and text, will choose how to bring interpretation to expression.

Imaging the Word may be used in a variety of ways: for your personal devotions, for devotions with others of different ages at home, as a resource for worship, preaching, or congregational life, or along with the other components of *Word Among Us: A Worship-centered, Lectionary-based Curriculum for Congregations.*

The following introductions will assist you in becoming an imaginative interpreter. The first article describes the spiritual discipline of contemplation as you consider three works of art. "God's Big Adventure" challenges older children and youth to imagine and pray. Parents and teachers may also discover skills to help younger children engage the Bible and art.

Draw deep. Imagine and question. Pray and act.

Sidney D. Fowler
Editor for Curriculum Resources
United Church Press

Imaging the Word represents a commitment to foster religious identity in individuals and communities, particularly Christian parishes and congregations. This volume, which is one component in the three-year comprehensive curriculum *Word Among Us: A Worship-centered, Lectionary-based Curriculum for Congregations,* is a prayerful, poetic, and visual resource that assists in fashioning identity.

Praying and Imaging: The Art of Contemplation

We do not have to be passive victims of a world that wants to entertain and distract us. We can make decisions and choices. A spiritual life in the midst of our energy-draining society requires us to take conscious steps to safeguard that inner space where we can keep our eyes fixed on the beauty of [Christ].

Henri Nouwen

Bagong Kussudiardja, *The Ascension*

As the twenty-first century approaches, media images and sound bites bombard our culture. The images are clever, seductive, and memorable, but they often obscure deeper truths about everything from global politics to the human need for advertised products. We are encouraged to accept commercially well-crafted pictures or words without much consideration of a deeper reality.

Imaging the Word: An Arts and Lectionary Resource offers an alternative to a superficial and hasty viewing of the world's images. It invites you to take the time to hold images—to study them, feel them, judge them. It invites you to go deeply into the stories of the Bible and into images and poetic text. It invites you to seek the Word beyond the sound bite, and to encounter the three-dimensional human truth beyond the image. It invites you into prayer.

The ancient spiritual discipline of *contemplation* is a form of prayer that requires setting aside a time and place in one's life and the life of a community to consider the presence of God in many and surprising manifestations. You are encouraged to slow down, to read, and to take time to be open to accounts from the Bible and companion images and poetic texts. You are invited to be open to God and to discover and connect Word with image, with words, and with your world.

Incarnation—The Living Word in the World

Imaging the Word takes as its starting place the incarnation: the wonderful event when God became human in Christ Jesus. In full humanity, Jesus revealed God. The stuff of the earth, including the human being, is one of the powerful arenas in which God creates, acts, saves, and loves. The arts are likewise an expression of God's incarnational activity. Edward Robinson in *The Language of Mystery* says:

> It should in fact be more natural for Christianity than for any other religious tradition to have a positive relationship with the arts, particularly those which, like painting or sculpture, pottery or weaving, draw directly on the material world for their means of expression. A conviction of the basic goodness of creation is built into the whole Judaic tradition: God looked upon [God's] work and saw it to be good. For a Christian, belief in the incarnation of the divine in the human figure of Christ reflects also an acceptance of the rest of creation as in some way embodying that same creative energy.

The incarnation means that God is discovered once again and calls out to us through our contemplation of and action in God's creative activity in our world. By prayerfully discerning the living Word revealed in Scripture and in the Spirit-inspired artistic witnesses of earth, we hear God speak.

Jonathan Green, *Tales*

Contemplation and Art—Entering the Bible Story

The arts can inform contemplative prayer in many ways. Sometimes stories, music, poetry, drama, and visual arts allow you to enter into and more deeply contemplate Bible stories. Whether the art is classical or contemporary, European or cross-cultural, whether it is a literal telling or an interpretive telling, try to enter the image and its unique account.

Take, for example, the depiction of the South African *griot,* or storyteller, in the painting *Tales.* The artist, Jonathan Green, places the storyteller at the foreground with his back to you, the viewer. In full view are the hearers of his story—and their farm, their dog, their walking staff, their lives. The storyteller and his story are the focus of the community. One person listens from his aerial post in an impressive tree. What role might the storyteller have in this rural, predominantly black community?

Although the painting does not literally depict the story of Jesus and Zacchaeus, it suggests the account in Luke 19:1–10. Read the story and then view the painting once again. Does imagining Jesus in this context raise any possibilities for you?

What does Green highlight in the painting? Which faces? What scenery? Which colors? The storyteller (Jesus, as imagined) has his back to the viewer of the painting. Is this troubling to you?

Noel Counihan, *Homage to Goya*
(Requiem for El Salvador)

Do you wish you could see his face? Can you, in your imagination, enter this image? Can you take different roles? Can you see the scene through Jesus' eyes? Take the place of a bystander or the man (Zacchaeus) in the tree. Can you converse with Jesus? Do new questions take shape in your mind because you are in the crowd of listeners? Are you surprised to find him where he is, doing what he is doing? Can you relate to the confusion of his followers or Zacchaeus?

Can you converse with this specific image of Jesus—not with a general picture of Jesus or with all the ideas about Jesus you have built up over the years? Can you converse with this Jesus, *griot*, teller of tales, whose stories call forth repentance and new life in Zacchaeus' life—right here in the moment captured in this painting? Consider, contemplate, and pray.

Contemplation and the Arts—Inspired Insight

Some of the art in *Imaging the Word* does not directly represent or illustrate a Bible reading. However, it may evoke a new insight about the reading or connect with your own life. Take, for example, Noel Counihan's *Homage to Goya (Requiem for El Salvador)*, which was chosen to accompany the unit for Proper 28 (page 70), "By Your Endurance." The Gospel reading for that week is Luke 21:5–19, in which Jesus teaches about the struggles that lie ahead for his followers.

Francisco Goya, *Third of May, 1808*

Counihan's image is disturbing in its simplicity—a man with his arms outstretched as if shot through the heart. The painting captures that last moment of terror. His clothing is ragged, his eyes full of fear. His plight, as the title of the painting suggests, was common to the Salvadoran poor and those who advocated for them during the years of political repression and death squads.

Contemplation of such an image connects you to the world. The pain and sorrow you see on the evening news become more stark and arresting when frozen on canvas. You are called to stop, look, think, and feel. The image gives vivid expression to words in any news report. Feelings of horror, or sadness, or rage at injustice may seize you, infiltrate your consciousness, take up abode in you.

The artist places this image in the context of another story of political repression, referring in his title to the central image in Francisco Goya's *Third of May, 1808*, which depicts a political execution during the Napoleonic Wars of the early nineteenth century. The subject of that painting has his arms outstretched as he receives a bullet to the heart. The posture of both Goya's and Counihan's figures points to the classic image of Jesus on the cross. The horror, the fear, the innocence of Jesus on the cross resonate in the image of the Salvadoran peasant dying, a victim of the sin that poisons his society.

In this deceptively simple image, you are called to understand the suffering and death of the Salvadoran through the lens of Jesus' death. At the same time, by seeing the pain so vividly on the Salvadoran's face, you are confronted with new insight into Jesus' suffering. As a Christian,

Graham Sutherland, *The Crucifixion*

you may be called to confront your hope of resurrection in the face of such suffering, and to consider anew the meaning of Jesus' teaching: "You will be betrayed even by parents and brothers, by relatives and friends; and they will put some of you to death. You will be hated by all because of my name. But not a hair of your head will perish. By your endurance you will gain your souls" (Luke 21:16–19).

By contemplating images and Bible readings with this depth of feeling, you may discover such insights and connect your faith, your hope, and your political beliefs.

Contemplation and the Arts—Prayer for Transformation

Prayer is a transforming activity. When you encounter God's Word, when you absorb it and open yourself to it, you risk change. Contemplation seeks deeper truth, the hope to which you are called, the justice to which the world is called, the vision of God's dominion to which all are called and which Jesus preached. Sincere contemplation, practiced over time, can change you. Make space in your life for God, for God's world, and you will find your relationship to that world changing as you discover connections that were overlooked before. You will find yourself engaged in God's world with your whole self—mind, heart, soul, strength.

For this kind of transformation to happen, more of yourself must be revealed during prayer. Present yourself to God. Ask intimate and challenging questions of God. While in prayer, you may also discover questions about yourself—about your limitations, struggles, dreams, fears. Like Jacob in the reading for Proper 13 (page 250), you may struggle intimately with God. Nothing is hidden before God. Love, forgiveness, and mercy invite you to change and to respond to God's great love.

Ellis Wilson's *Funeral Procession* (see next page; suggested to be viewed alongside the Epistle reading from 2 Thessalonians 2:16–17 for Proper 27 on page 66) is an image that may help you present yourself to God. Given its title, you might find yourself surprised by the hope the painting may bring. In it a long line of people walk along a winding path to a funeral. Women, dressed plainly in black, white, or gray, with covered heads, carry flowers. What conveys hope? Is it the lush green surrounding them? the beautiful red clay path they follow? Is it the deliberation and serenity with which they seem to move? Or is there hope because the woman in the foreground, at the center of the composition, is so obviously pregnant, and surrounded by children?

Who has died? Who is the person for whom they so calmly process? The painting gives no clue. The line does not reach the church or cemetery. In fact, it has no beginning or end. The mourners do not have individual features in their faces. Is this disturbing to you? Or does this lead you to look at the procession as a whole? There is a sense that the entire community has turned out for the funeral.

Ellis Wilson, *Funeral Procession*

What is the pregnant woman moving toward? Toward someone's burial? Toward her own death? She is clearly moving more deeply into life as she moves toward the delivery of her baby, who will take its place in the beautiful procession.

Imagine yourself in the painting. Where are you—at the head of the line or hanging back? Do you want to be near the expectant mother, a sign of new life amidst other signs of life? Where are you in the journey between birth and death? Do you journey with hope and joy? Where is your hope?

Funeral Procession was chosen as a visual meditation for the reading from 2 Thessalonians for the unit titled "Eternal Comfort, Good Hope." The march of the mourners conveys a sense of marching into the future—the grave included. Yet the procession seems to reinforce the knowledge that the people of God have eternal hope. Togetherness, beauty, new life, community—the procession of human beings through their mortality is ultimately hopeful.

As you contemplate the painting and the readings, what words of comfort and judgment do you perceive? Your perception may reveal truth about yourself and your own hopes and dreams. You may be led to transformation and to live out those hopes.

Enjoy *Imaging the Word: An Arts and Lectionary Resource*. Take the time to contemplate alone or with others. Consider the images in relation to the stories of God. Enter more deeply into your world, your faith, your community, your self. Proceed with courage to the deeper reality that is God, leading you and God's people to grow, to risk, and to contribute to a future of love and justice you can only imagine, but in which you confidently believe.

Susan A. Blain
Catherine O'Callaghan

God's Big World—An Adventure for Young People

Carmen Lomas Garza, *Camas para sueños*
(*Beds for Dreams*)

Let the colorful pages of *Imaging the Word* lead you on an adventure—an adventure with God. You will journey by way of your imagination through Bible stories about God and God's people. Accompanying the stories are images, poems, prayers, and words that have been carefully chosen to help you enter into adventures with God's big world.

As in some adventures, you will pass through familiar territory where you will encounter familiar people and places. You may read the prayer "Now I Lay Me Down to Sleep" and say, "I've heard that before." You may have heard the story of the Magi over and over, and seen the *Peanuts* cartoon on page 117. You may have read, heard, or seen things from this book on television, in movies, in other books, in museums, or in your neighborhood.

Adventures are also full of surprises, however, and these may open a door to an unseen world. *Imaging the Word* will let you discover new people, places, and times. You may even need to do some detective work to understand the Bible stories, the words, or the pictures. Some of the images you will encounter will be beautiful and musical, and some will disturb or confuse you. Yet when you return from these adventures, you may discover that you have changed.

You may see things differently.

You may not quite be the same person you were before.

Your world may have become larger.

Your relationship and friendship with God may have deepened.

You can travel this adventure alone or with family or friends. Talk with others about your thoughts, questions, and feelings. Browse anytime through *Imaging the Word* or set aside time once a week throughout the year. Be willing to ask questions, and to recognize that there will rarely be just one answer. Use the God-given gift of your imagination as you embark on this adventure.

Before you start, you may want to practice looking at some of the images or pictures. Because some of the material in *Imaging the Word* will be unfamiliar to you, in this section we present examples of the art, as well as some questions for you to consider as you begin to look at the images.

Giotto, *Entry into Jerusalem*

Some Images Tell a Story from the Bible

Images like Giotto's *Entry into Jerusalem* are great for telling stories from the Bible. When you find pictures of Bible stories, ask questions.

Ask general questions. What is happening in this picture? What moment in the story does the artist include? What feelings do the faces and bodies of the people express? What feelings do the colors, light, and shapes convey? What other discoveries or questions come to mind?

Ask specific questions.
Put yourself in the picture!
Play all the parts.

You are Jesus, riding the donkey through the crowd. Look closely at Jesus. What are you thinking? What are you feeling? Are you surprised? worried about the future? sad?

You are one of Jesus' disciples, following behind him as he enters Jerusalem. He has told you he has to die here. What are you thinking about? How do you feel? What do you think of this crowd of people?

You are one of the crowd. Are you standing, or have you climbed a tree to watch the procession? Are you shouting "Hosanna!" with the others? What do you think about the man on the donkey? What is it like to be at such an event?

Sometimes it's fun to imagine that you are something other than a person in the picture. If you could talk and you were a palm branch, or a donkey, or the road that Jesus is traveling on, what would you say?

Read the story from the Bible. Find the verses in the Bible, or get someone to help you find them. The verses are listed in each unit. As you read Matthew 21:1–11, does the painting match the story? What is different? What questions do you have about the Bible story? After reading the story, would you change your answers to any of the earlier questions?

Tell God about your adventure. After looking at the picture and reading the story, take time for prayer. Try to be quiet for a while and then tell God what you discovered. If you wish, talk to a friend or family member about your thoughts.

Some Images Depict Ordinary People in Their Everyday Lives

Some images in this book are scenes from the lives of everyday people. God speaks through the experiences of their everyday lives as God may speak through the stories of the Bible.

Rembrandt's *Two Women Teaching a Child to Walk* was chosen to accompany the unit "By Your Endurance" (page 70), which explores how people gain strength and experience God during hard times.

Rembrandt Harmensz van Rijn,
Two Women Teaching a Child to Walk

The way you enter this picture adventure is similar to the way you enter a story picture. However, the questions are a bit different.

**Ask general questions. What is happening in this picture?
What feelings are expressed by the way the people are drawn?
What do you think the artist used to draw the picture?**

Ask specific questions. Use your imagination. As you look at the image, think about each character.

What is the experience—the child's learning to walk—like for each person in the picture? Is it easy or hard for the child to walk? What kind of time is the child in this picture having? What kind of time are the adults having? Can you make up a story about the picture?

Recall a similar experience. As you look at this image, think about what it's like to learn to walk or to learn anything new. Perhaps you have watched or helped a child learn to walk. What do you recall about that experience? Was it easy or hard for the child? Did the child learn quickly or over a long period of time? What feelings did the child express? Anger? Impatience? Excitement? Joy? Was it easy or hard to be the person helping the child? What qualities does a good helper need? Now that you are older, what experiences have you had that are similar to learning to walk?

Talk about God and your own adventure. How might faith in God be like learning to walk? Read Luke 21:5–19. Why might the Rembrandt drawing have been chosen to explore the theme "By Your Endurance"? Be quiet for a moment and then in a prayer tell God what discoveries you have made.

Some Images Don't Tell Any Story at All

Paintings like Gottlieb's *Apaquogue* do not depict people, objects, or scenes that give us clues to their subjects. Such paintings are called "abstracts." Other abstract paintings, like Pablo Picasso's *Woman Crying* on page 205, hint of something lifelike, such as the weeping figure, but emphasize shapes or color. Sometimes artists paint forms and colors that bring to mind feelings or meanings rather than a particular person, place, or event. Artists may not have any one meaning in mind when they paint such a picture. Again you may use the same steps in an abstract adventure, but the questions may differ.

Put yourself in the picture.

What would it be like to be the child?

one of the adults?

Adolph Gottlieb, *Apaquogue*

Ask general questions. What forms and colors did the artist use? Do the forms seem to move or stand still? Are they "quiet" or do they seem to "shout"?

How do the colors or forms relate to one another? Are they alike or different?

Ask specific questions of yourself. Use your imagination. What do you feel and think as you look at the colors and forms? What kind of movement, energy, or spirit do the colors and shapes suggest to you? If you look at the image for a long time, what do you find yourself thinking about?

Express your picture adventure to God. Why do you suppose this image was chosen to explore the unit "God's Spirit Poured Out" (page 54)? Read Joel 2:28–29. Using markers or crayons or whatever materials you have available, create your own abstract artwork on the theme "God's Spirit Poured Out." What colors and forms can you use to express the Spirit? Once again, be quiet for a moment or so, then tell God any discoveries you have made during your abstract adventure.

Exploring the Bible through the arts is indeed an adventure. You meet people, go places, and do and feel things that are new and that challenge you. Your world will continue to expand as you learn more and more about the world of the Bible and of artists. Share your adventures and your discoveries with family and friends.

May God's adventure in our world become your own exciting, loving, and faithful adventure.

Sharon Gouwen

Pentecost <hr/> (Cycle C)

Jonathan Green, *Tales*, detail

<hr/>
20

We grow in grace, slowly,

unremarkably,

ordinarily, yet miraculously.

The longest season of the liturgical year follows Pentecost, a season known in some traditions as ordinary time. It is the season when the church studies and reflects on the teachings of Jesus and the implications for our own lives. What is discipleship in the ordinary?

We listen carefully to Jesus in ordinary time; we accompany him in his travels. What is there about this teacher that would send small Zacchaeus up into a tree to see him, then catapult him down into Jesus' presence and on into a new relationship of justice with his neighbors?

We puzzle over his parables. Who is this most ordinary of characters, a housekeeper sweeping, and what is her precious lost coin? Can Jesus be using this homely image to talk about God and us?

We meet his friends, his opponents, his questioners. We enter the story ourselves over and over, taking different roles, sympathetic first to this disciple, then to that person in need.

We grow in grace, slowly, unremarkably, ordinarily, yet miraculously. The color of the season of Pentecost is green, the color which in nature signals that earth, air, water, and sunlight have combined in their ordinary, unremarkable, yet miraculous way to produce growth and foster life.

DISCIPLESHIP IN THE ORDINARY

INVITE THE FORGOTTEN

Jesus said also to the person who had invited him, "When you give a luncheon or a dinner, do not invite your friends or your brother or sister or your relatives or rich neighbors, in case they may invite you in return, and you would be repaid. But when you give a banquet, invite those who are poor, crippled, lame, and blind."

Luke 14:12–13

Jack Baron, *The Picnic*

Sunday dinner, as we called it, was the best meal of the week. Mother fixed her finest foods, and my father, able to relax with the sermon delivered, livened the table conversation with his stories. The visitors who came to our table—some from next door, and some from around the globe—brought their own stories, pushing back the boundaries of our small world.

Years later I traveled to Honduras as a college student in an international study service program. There I found myself in the home of another pastor in another small village. This time the table was turned, I was the guest, and the hospitality I received was of a variety I had never before encountered. . . .

Doña Lillan's table was not large enough and she did not have enough dishes to feed the entire family at one time. But she graciously served food to any who stopped by at mealtime. . . .

I thought I knew what it meant to be hospitable and generous before I went to Honduras, but the Alemán family taught me much more. To learn from them required the uncomfortable task of simply being a guest and receiving their sacrificial gifts.

Joetta Handrich Schlabach, *Extending the Table*

Feast of Life

Come on.
Let us celebrate the supper of the Lord.
Let us make a huge loaf of bread
and let us bring abundant wine like at the
wedding at Cana.

Let the women not forget the salt.
Let the men bring along the yeast.
Let many guests come,
the lame, the blind, the crippled, the poor.

Come quickly.
Let us follow the recipe of the Lord.
All of us, let us knead the dough together
with our hands.
Let us see with joy how the bread grows.

Because today
we celebrate
the meeting with the Lord.
Today we renew our commitment
to the kingdom.
Nobody will stay hungry.

Elsa Tamez

Love Bade Me Welcome

Love bade me welcome: yet my soul drew back,
　　Guilty of dust and sin.
But quick-ey'd Love, observing me grow slack
　　From my first entrance in,
Drew nearer to me, sweetly questioning
　　If I lack'd anything.

A guest, I answer'd, worthy to be here:
　　Love said, you shall be he.
I the unkind, ungrateful? Ah, my dear,
　　I cannot look on thee.
Love took my hand, and smiling did reply,
　　Who made the eyes but I?

Truth Lord, but I have marr'd them: let my shame
　　Go where it doth deserve.
And know you not, says Love, who bore the blame?
　　My dear, then I will serve.
You must sit down, says Love, and taste my meat.
　　So I did sit and eat.

George Herbert

Kathryn Abbe, *Tea Party*

We're gonna sit at the welcome table.
We're gonna sit at the welcome table
  one of these days, hallelujah!
We're gonna sit at the welcome table.
We're gonna sit at the welcome table
  one of these days.

Traditional Spiritual

Edward Hopper, *Nighthawks*

The alienation of modern urban life is suggested in Hopper's *Nighthawks*. The shadowy apartment buildings and shopfronts in the background appear gloomy and silent; the only light seems to be coming from the all-night diner. The weariness and passivity of the patrons contrast with the energy of the soda jerk who serves them, as he creates a space of hospitality in a threatening, lonely city.

FEARFULLY AND WONDERFULLY MADE

Psalm 139:1-6, 13-18

praise you,

for I am fearfully

and wonderfully made.

Psalm 139:14a

O God, you have searched me and known me!

You know when I sit down and when I rise up;
you discern my thoughts from afar.

You search out my path and my lying down,
and are acquainted with all my ways.

Even before a word is on my tongue,
O God, you know it altogether.

You beset me behind and before,
and lay your hand upon me.

Such knowledge is too wonderful for me;
it is high, I cannot attain it.

For you formed my inward parts,
you knit me together in my mother's womb.

I praise you, for you are fearful and wonderful.
Wonderful are your works!
You know me right well;

my frame was not hidden from you,
when I was being made in secret,
intricately wrought in the depths of the earth.

Your eyes beheld my unformed substance;
in your book they were written, every one of them,
the days that were formed for me,
when as yet there was none of them.

How precious to me are your thoughts, O God!
How vast the sum of them!

If I would count them, they are more than the sand.
When I awake, I am still with you.

Jacob Lawrence, *And God created man and woman*, *Genesis Series 7*

In each painting of Lawrence's *Genesis Series*, he portrays the impassioned preacher's vision of creation. The sermon comes alive. Man and woman are created outside the windows in the imagination of the congregation.

Grandfather took us out
long after dark
and set his telescope up on the lawn
and showed us how to look through the lens.
We saw the mountains of the moon!
We saw the rings around Saturn!
We saw the stars in the Milky Way—
too many to count!
"See," Grandfather said,
"what wonders God has made!"
And then he hugged each one of us
and said, "And you are wondrous, too!"

Madeleine L'Engle

Carmen Lomas Garza, *Camas para Sueños (Beds for Dreams)*

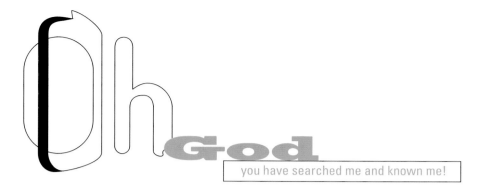

Oh God

you have searched me and known me!

Soil for legs
Axe for hands
Flower for eyes
Bird for ears
Mushroom for nose
Smile for mouth
Songs for lungs
Sweat for skin
Wind for mind
Just enough.

Nanao Sakaki

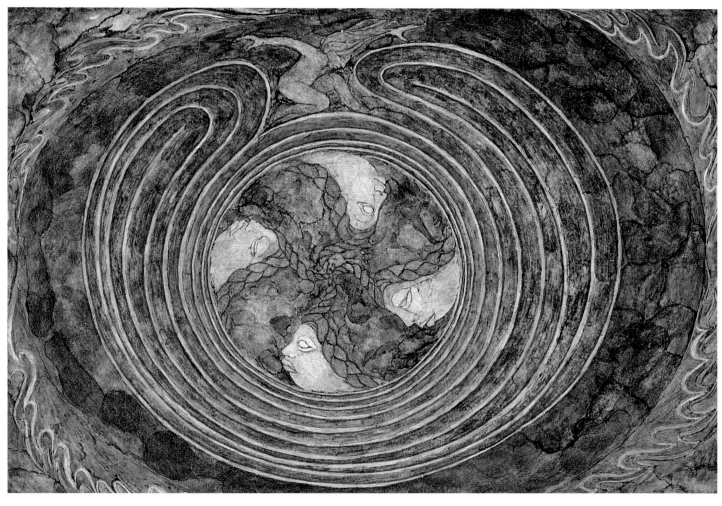

Meinrad Craighead, *Changing Woman*

The dream images of Meinrad Craighead often open the way to imagining the process of change—of fetus in womb; of psyche developing toward maturity; of the imagination itself making connections and growing.

S E E K ,   F I N D ,   R E J O I C E

When the woman has

found the coin, she calls

together her friends and

neighbors saying,

"Rejoice with me,

I have found the coin

that I had lost."

Luke 15:9

lady in red
i waz missin somethin

lady in purple
somethin so important

lady in orange
somethin promised

lady in blue
a layin on of hands

lady in green
fingers near my forehead

lady in yellow
strong

lady in green
cool

lady in orange
movin

lady in purple
makin me whole

     ...

lady in purple
not my mama / holdin me tight / sayin
i'm always gonna be her girl
not a layin on of bosom & womb
a layin on of hands
the holiness of myself released

lady in red
i sat up one nite walkin a boardin house
screamin / cryin / the ghost of another woman
who waz missin what i waz missin
i wanted to jump up outta my bones
& be done wit myself . . .
til the only tree i cd see
took me up in her branches
held me in the breeze
made me dawn dew
that chill at daybreak
the sun wrapped me up swingin rose light everywhere
the sky laid over me like a million men
i waz cold / i waz burnin up / a child
& endlessly weavin garments for the moon
wit my tears

i found god in myself
& i loved her / i loved her fiercely

All of the ladies repeat to themselves softly
the lines 'i found god in myself & i loved her.'
It soon becomes a song of joy. . . .

Ntozake Shange, from *A Choreopoem: For Colored Girls*
Who Have Considered Suicide/When the Rainbow Is Enuf

Jean Édouard Vuillard, *Woman Sweeping*

The woman seeking the precious lost coin portrays God as an ordinary housekeeper employed in the most ordinary of daily, life-sustaining routines.

Bud Lee, *Reverend Howard Finster's "Paradise Garden" in Summerville, Georgia*

With scraps and thrown-away junk Finster creates his vision of Eden.
It glitters with biblical texts made of bits of broken mirrors embedded
in the walls and walks.

I searched

far and

I was passionate,

filled with longing,

I searched

far and wide.

But the day

that the Truthful One

found me,

I was at home.

Lal Ded, 14th century, Kashmir

Now I must write for myself   for this blind
woman scratching the pavement   with her wand of thought
this slippered crone   inching on icy streets
reaching into wire trashbaskets   pulling out
what was thrown away   and infinitely precious

I look at my hands and see   they are still unfinished
I look at the vine and see the leafbud
inching towards life

I look at my face in the glass   and see
a halfborn woman

1975

Adrienne Rich, excerpt from "Upper Broadway"

wide...

GRIEVE WITH GOD

Pablo Picasso, *Guernica*

Shortly after Hitler's forces bombed this small Basque village during the Spanish Civil War, Pablo Picasso was commissioned by the Spanish Loyalist government to paint this mural for the Paris World's Fair of 1937. Various interpretations have been offered for this work. Pain, dismay, despair, and anguish mark the six human faces as well as that of the horse.

ark, the cry of my poor people from far and wide in the land: "Is God not in Zion? Is Zion's Ruler not there?" (Why have they provoked me to anger with their images, with their foreign idols?)

Jeremiah 8:19

Around me people were praying, and some stretched out their arms in the form of a cross, imploring mercy from Heaven.

The sound of the explosions and of the crumbling houses cannot be imagined. . . . The new bombardment lasted thirty-five minutes, sufficient to transform the town into an enormous furnace.

Not even the people who went into the refuges were saved; nor the sick and wounded in the hospitals.

When the bombing was over, the people left their shelters. I saw no one crying. Stupor was written on all their faces.

When it grew dark the flames of Guernika were reaching to the sky, and the clouds took on the color of blood, and our faces too shone with the color of blood.

"Guernika," in *The Civil War in Spain, 1936–1939*, ed. Robert Payne

Holy God,
holy and strange,
holy and intimate,
have mercy on us.

O my people, what have I done to you?
How have I offended you?
Answer me.

I brooded over the abyss,
with my words I called forth creation:
but you have brooded on destruction,
and manufactured the means of chaos.

O my people, what have I done to you?
How have I offended you?
Answer me.

I breathed life into your bodies,
and carried you tenderly in my arms:
but you have armed yourselves for war,
breathing out threats of violence.

O my people, what have I done to you?
How have I offended you?
Answer me.

. . .

I abandoned my power like a garment,
choosing your unprotected flesh:
but you have robed yourself in privilege,
and chosen to despise the abandoned.

O my people, what have I done to you?
How have I offended you?
Answer me.

Holy God,
holy and strange,
holy and intimate,
have mercy on us.

I would have gathered you to me as a lover,
and shown you the ways of peace:
but you desired security,
and you would not surrender yourself.

O my people, what have I done to you?
How have I offended you?
Answer me.

. . .

I have followed you with the power of my spirit,
to seek the truth and heal the oppressed:
but you have been following a lie,
and returned to your own comfort.

O my people, what have I done to you?
How have I offended you?
Answer me.

Holy God,
holy and strange,
holy and intimate,
have mercy on us.

Janet Morley

The liturgy on the preceding page is a contemporary example of the "Reproaches," which are traditionally sung as part of the Good Friday liturgy. They are a dialogue between a grieving God who recounts the many ways in which humanity turns from God's love, and a people who respond with a cry for mercy. The traditional reproaches have often been interpreted as anti-Semitic, insofar as they juxtapose the mighty acts of God in the Hebrew Scriptures with the rejection of Jesus and his death on the cross in such a way as to blame the Jews for this death. Janet Morley's contemporary version corrects this by juxtaposing the mighty acts of God in both the Hebrew and the Christian Scriptures with the manifestations of sin in human life that consistently turn humanity from God.

There Is a Balm in Gilead

There is a balm in Gilead to make the wounded whole.

There is a balm in Gilead to heal the sin-sick soul.

Sometimes I feel discouraged,

and think my work's in vain,

But then the Holy Spirit revives my soul again.

Don't ever feel discouraged,

For Jesus is your friend,

And if you lack for knowledge,

He'll not refuse to lend.

If you cannot preach like Peter,

If you cannot pray like Paul,

You can tell the love of Jesus

And say, "He died for all."

African American Spiritual

Rembrandt Harmensz van Rijn, *Jeremiah Lamenting the Destruction of Jerusalem* (opposite)

The source of human pain is often human sinfulness, as the passage from Jeremiah indicates. Image and text give voice to the world's pain. Provoked by our disobedience, God nevertheless does not withdraw from us. Like Jeremiah lamenting the destruction of Israel, God weeps for us.

THE WAY OF FAITH

Pursue righteousness, godliness, faith, love, endurance, gentleness. Fight the good fight of the faith; take hold of the eternal life, to which you were called.

1 Timothy 6:11b–12a

The weapons of our warfare are not material ones,

. . . but . . . they are mighty in leveling fortifications,

foiling stratagems, and reducing every tower erected

against the wisdom of God. You will find . . . the Lord's harness,

with which you can resist in the day of evil.

You will find the weapons of justice on the right hand and on the left;

you will find truth, the cover for your body,

the breastplate of justice and the shield of faith,

upon which you can extinguish all the fiery missiles of malignant Satan.

You will find the helmet of righteousness

and the sword of the spirit, which is the Word of God.

Erasmus

Evil, sin, and death were ever-present and very palpable realities for medieval women and men, as Erasmus' words and Dürer's image reveal. Corruption, warfare, disease, and death were constants in medieval daily life. To us, the metaphor of the Christian soldier may seem strange and out of place, even inappropriate. For them, it was a powerful way to visualize how they, armed with God's grace, were to combat the physical and spiritual forces that assailed them.

Albrecht Dürer,
Knight, Death, and the Devil

This image is sometimes interpreted as the Christian knight who fights against death (holding the hour glass) and the devil (horned, holding a spear).

HEART AND MOUTH AND DEED AND LIFE

MUST BEAR WITNESS TO CHRIST

WITHOUT FEAR OR HYPOCRISY.

J. S. BACH

Eric Miller, *South African Demonstration*

In July 1992, South African black school children confronted riot police during a demonstration outside of a white-only school.
After several demonstrations, they were allowed equal access to education.

[A gift] my mother has given me is the understanding *La vida es la lucha*—The struggle is life. For over half my life I thought my task was to struggle and then one day I would enjoy the fruits of my labor. This is the kind of resignation and expectation of being rewarded in the next life that the . . . Church has taught for centuries. Then I began to reflect on what my mother often tells the family: "All we need to ask of God is to have health and strength to struggle. As long as we have what we need to struggle in life, we need ask for nothing else." This understanding gives me much strength in my everyday life. It has allowed me to be realistic—to understand that, for the vast majority of women, life is an ongoing struggle. But above all it has made me realize that I can and should relish the struggle. The struggle is my life; my dedication to the struggle is one of the main driving forces in my life.

Ada María Isasi-Díaz

The disciple is dragged out of . . . relative security
    into a life of absolute insecurity . . . ,
out of the realm of finite . . .
    into the realm of infinite possibilities.

Dietrich Bonhoeffer

Have mercy
Upon us.
Have mercy
Upon our efforts,
That we
Before Thee,
in love and in faith,
Righteousness and humility,
May follow Thee,
With self-denial, steadfastness,
   and courage,
And meet Thee
In the silence.

Give us
A pure heart
That we may see Thee,
A humble heart
That we may hear Thee,
A heart of love
That we may serve Thee,
A heart of faith
That we may live Thee,
Thou
Whom I do not know
But Whose I am.

Thou
Whom I do not comprehend
But Who hast dedicated me
To my fate.
Thou—

Dag Hammarskjöld

A GRANDMOTHER'S FAITH

I am reminded of your sincere faith, a faith that lived first in your grandmother Lois and your mother Eunice and now, I am sure, lives in you. For this reason I remind you to rekindle the gift of God that is within you through the laying on of my hands; for God did not give us a spirit of cowardice, but rather a spirit of power and of love and of self-discipline.

2 Timothy 1:5–7

Archibald J. Motley, Jr., *Mending Socks* (opposite)

They went together—those wrinkled hands and tattered book. And something in the awe with which she held it made me think she held a sacred fire.

The old brass-bound Bible came to her from her mother, and hers before that, too, through more generations than I know how to reckon—faded, cracked, worn with use.

I wonder how it felt to hold the past within her hands— how many broken hearts found comfort there, how many searching minds were fed; how many fears were calmed in its reading; what songs of joy were hummed over it; what secret tears still stain its pages?

I loved to hear her talk to God, and when she prayed, I sometimes imagined I felt God near. It was a very safe place to be—with God and her. I liked her God, so wrapped up in the small goings-on of daily life—not too far away and busy with eternal things to take notice of one small child.

The Bible became mine today, and my smooth hands look somehow out of place—and somehow right at home. Like her, I hold the accumulated joys and sorrows of my heritage and join my life with theirs. There is a strength to it—forged by faithful living in the presence of a loving God. The line still holds—all those who have gone before, myself, and those who are to come.

Marie Livingston Roy

A faith that

first lived

This genealogy of mothers' names

is based on the genealogy

found in the Gospel of Matthew,

where only the names of

the fathers are recorded.

A genealogy of Jesus Christ, the son of Miriam,
the daughter of Anna:
Sarah was the mother of Isaac,
and Rebekah was the mother of Jacob,
Leah was the mother of Judah,
Tamar was the mother of Perez.
The names of the mothers of Hezron, Ram, Amminadab,
Nahshon and Salmon have been lost.
Rehab was the mother of Boaz,
and Ruth was the mother of Obed.
Obed's wife, whose name is unknown, bore Jesse.
The wife of Jesse was the mother of David.
Bathsheba was the mother of Solomon,
Na'amah, the Ammonitess, was the mother of Rehoboam.
Ma'acah was the mother of Abijah and Asa.
Azubah was the mother of Ahaziah,
Zibia of Beersheba, the mother of Jehoash.
Jecoliah of Jerusalem bore Uzziah,
Jerushah bore Jotham; Ahaz's mother is unknown.
Abijah was the mother of Hezekiah,
Hephzibah was the mother of Manasses,
Meshullemeth was the mother of Amon,
Jedidah was the mother of Josiah.
Zebidah was the mother of Jehoiakim,
Nehushta was the mother of Johoiakin,
Hamutal was the mother of Zedekiah.
Then the deportation to Babylon took place.
After the deportation to Babylon
the names of the mothers go unrecorded.
These are their sons:
Jechoniah, Shealtiel, Zerubbabel,
Abiud, Eliakim, Azor and Zadok,
Achim, Eliud, Eleazar,
Matthan, Jacob, and
Joseph, the husband of Miriam.
Of her was born Jesus who is called Christ.
The sum of generations is therefore:
fourteen from Sarah to David's mother;
fourteen from Bathsheba to the Babylonian deportation;
and fourteen from the Babylonian deportation to Miriam,
the mother of Christ.

Women's Liturgy Group of New York

A Song of Greatness

Telling of heroes,
Telling of great deeds
Of ancient days,
When I hear them telling,
Then I think within me
I too am one of these.

When I hear the people
Praising great ones,
Then I know I too
Shall be esteemed,
I too when my time comes
Shall do mightily.

Translated by Mary Austin
A Chippewa Indian Song

Rick Reinhard, *Laying on of Hands*

The Faith of the Bible's Timothy

Faith is what is handed down from mother to daughter to son, but not merely as a package passed from one generation to another, but as "a faith which was alive" in mother and daughter and which now lives in the child of the third generation.

Carl R. Holladay

GOD'S AWESOME DEEDS

All the earth worships you;

they sing praises to you,

sing praises to your name.

Come and see what God has

done; God does awesome

deeds among mortals.

Psalm 66:4–5

Thanksgiving psalms speak of the personal experience of a new order.... Surprises and newness overcome the old way of looking at the world.... Thanksgivings tell the story of the past distress and of God's saving reversal of the situation.... [They] give testimony for conversion. In telling our story of wonder and awe, we are evangelists, calling people to a life of faith in this God who has saved us.

Denise Dombkowski Hopkins

Linda Lomahaftewa, *New Mexico Sunset*

As the psalmist begins Psalm 66 with a call for "joyful noise to God," it is not simply a call to Israel. It is a call to "all the earth." God is not only Israel's God. God is the awesome creator of all things and all peoples. . . . To sing glory to God's name is to sing glory to God's being and all God stands for.

Paul Hammer

CANTICLE OF THE SUN

Wakantanka Taku Nitawa
Many and Great, O God, Are Your Works

Wakantanka taku nitawa
tankaya qa ota,
Mahpiya kin eyahnake ça,
maka kin he duowanca,
Mniowanca ´sbeya wanke cin,
hena oyakihi.

Woehdaku nitawa kin he
minagi kin qu wo;
Mahpiya kin iwankam yati,
wicowa´ste yuha nanka,
Wiconi kin he mayaqu nun,
owihanke wanin.

Many and great, O God, are your works,
Maker of earth and sky;
Your hands have set the heavens with stars,
your fingers spread the mountains and plains.
Lo, at your word the waters were formed;
Deep seas obey your voice.

Grant unto us communion with you,
O star abiding One;
Come unto us and dwell with us:
With you are found the gifts of life.
Bless us with life that has no end,
Eternal life with you.

Joseph R. Renville (paraphrased by R. Philip Frazier)

Be praised, my God,
for all your creatures,
and first for brother sun,
who makes the day bright and luminous.
And he is beautiful and radiant
    with great splendor,
he is the image of you, Most High.

Be praised, my God,
for sister moon and the stars,
in the sky you have made them brilliant and precious and beautiful.

Be praised, my God, for brother wind
and for the air both cloudy and serene
    and every kind of weather,
through which you give nourishment to your creatures.

Be praised, my God, for sister water,
who is very useful and humble
    and precious and chaste.

Be praised, my God, for brother fire,
through whom you illuminate the night.
And he is beautiful and joyous and robust and strong.

Be praised, my God, for our sister, mother earth,
    who . . . watches over us
and brings forth various fruits
    with colored flowers and herbs.

Be praised, my God,
    for our sister, bodily death,
from whom no living thing can escape.
Blessed are those whom she finds doing your most holy will. . . .

Praise and bless my God
and give thanks to God and serve God
    with great humility.
One instant is eternity;
eternity is the now.
When you see through this one instant,
you see through the one who sees.

St. Francis of Assisi (1182 – 1226)

Michael Kabotie, *Petroglyphs*

The painting based on the rock-painted artistry of ancient people portrays the interaction between creatures and humans from the beginning of humankind.

WORDS, SWEETER THAN HONEY

How sweet are your words to my taste, sweeter than honey to my mouth! Through your precepts I get understanding; therefore I hate every false way.

Psalm 119:103–104

Joel Mayes, a deaf boy
twelve years old,
saw the man brought in
and knew it was a dead man,
but his eyes were for
something else,
something wonderful.
He saw the breaths coming
out of people's mouths,
and his dark face,
losing just now a little of
its softness, showed its
secret desire. It was
marvelous to him when
the infinite designs
of speech became visible
in formations on the air,
and he watched with
awe that changed to tenderness
whenever people met and
passed in the road with
an exchange of words.

Eudora Welty

Wilmer Jennings, *De Good Book Says*

All words are spiritual—nothing is more spiritual than words.—
Whence are they? along how many thousands and tens of thousands of years have they come?
those eluding, fluid, beautiful, fleshless, realities,
Mother, Father, Water, Earth, Me, This, Soul, Tongue, House, Fire.
What beauty there is in words! What a lurking curious charm in the sound of some words!

Walt Whitman

I read the Torah as Jews have read it and loved it for centuries. For example, I can tell you what is the middle word in the Torah. I can tell you what is the middle letter in the Torah. Over the generations Jewish scholars have read the Torah not as a novel to see how it ends, but as a love letter. For instance,"Why did he use this word instead of that word?" "Why is there a space here?" "Why a comma here instead of a period?" That's the way you read a love letter and wonder, "What did he or she mean by this word?" We Jews have seen the Torah as not just a book of stories or law codes, but as a love letter from God.

Harold Kushner, in *Questions of Faith*

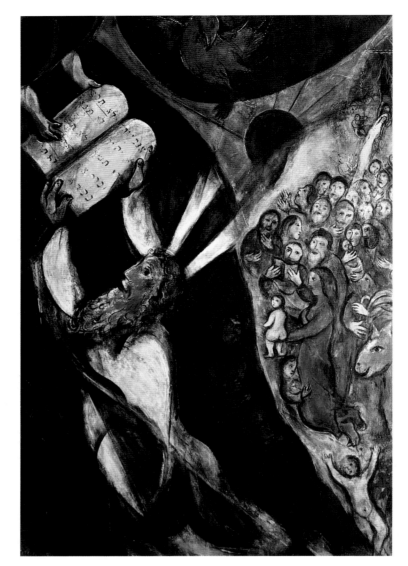

Marc Chagall, *Moses Receiving the Tablets of the Law*

the word

"we want to love and don't know how"

I love you

Bless me, son, for I have sinned the sin of too many fathers who do not tell sons how much they love them. . . . Of course, Bill, I thought it a couple of millions times, but unless it is said aloud, how would you, how could you really know? . . . Love is not just what you do, it is also what you say. Hearing is also believing. . . . Damn it, Bill, I knew better. Was I not taught and did I not teach again and again that our human condition is that "we want to love and don't know how." Why did this father not learn what he knew? Yes, of course, it was the Word that was made flesh, but it was the Word that was made flesh in words, spoken words.

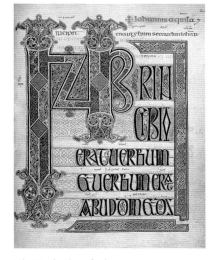

The Book of Lindesfarne,
detail of the first letter of John's Gospel

Bless me, son, for I have sinned. I never learned how to just say "I love you, son," lovingly enough, loudly enough.

Anderson Clark *This excerpt is from a father's letter to his son dying of AIDS.*

made flesh

GOD'S SPIRIT POURED OUT

Then afterward I will pour out my spirit on all flesh; your sons and daughters shall prophesy, your old men shall dream dreams, and your young men shall see visions. Even on the male and female slaves, in those days, I will pour out my spirit.

Joel 2:28–29

The Holy Spirit is life that gives life,
Moving all things.
It is the root in every creature
And purifies all things,
Wiping away our sins, anointing wounds.
It is radiant life, worthy of praise,
Awakening and enlivening all things.

Hildegard of Bingen

John Pitman Weber, *Yell*

John Pitman Weber works at creating an "art of Social Conscience" rooted in liberation theology's vision of hope amidst struggle for justice.

[Joel] speaks of a terrible plague of locusts.... In its utter destruction this attack symbolizes for him the coming Day of the Lord—"a...gloomy day."

But Joel brings a message of hope. If only Israel will repent and turn back to God, [who] is able to "restore the years that the locust has eaten."

Joel paints a wonderful picture of a coming day of God's blessing, when [the] Spirit will be abroad in the world.

Mary Batchelor

Adolph Gottlieb, *Apaquogue*

While artists like abstract expressionist painter Adolph Gottlieb often do not intend specific meanings for their paintings, the strength of the interplay of color and line in this painting may delight, energize, or challenge the viewer and offer an experience of Spirit in the world.

Litany

Glory to you, Almighty God!

    You spoke, and light came out of darkness,

    order rose from confusion.

Women: *You breathed into dust of the earth,*

    and we were formed in your image.

Men: *You looked on the work of your hands,*

    and declared that it was all good.

    And still you speak, breathe and look for us.

    We praise you!

    Glory to you, Holy Spirit!

    You brooded over chaos,

    mothering and shaping God's new creation.

Women: *You inspired prophets and evangelists*

    to discover the right word for the right season.

Men: *You liberated the early church for mission,*

    claiming all of life for the Lord of all.

    And still you brood over, inspire and liberate us.

    We praise you!

The Iona Community Worship Book

Great soaring Spirit,

sweeping in uncharted flight

across the bounds of time and space,

you fill the outflung galaxies

and move through earth's long centuries

with aching, mending, dancing grace.

Brian Wren

REMEMBER THE FAITHFUL

Praise God! Sing to God a new song, God's praise in the assembly of the faithful. For God takes pleasure in God's people; God adorns the humble with victory. Let the faithful exult in glory; let them sing for joy on their couches.

Psalm 149:1, 4–5

I THINK CONTINUALLY OF THOSE WHO WERE TRULY GREAT

Near the snow, near the sun, in the highest fields,
See how these names are feted by the waving grass
And by the streamers of white cloud
And whispers of wind in the listening sky,
The names of those who in their lives fought for life,

Who wore at their hearts the fire's centre.
Born of the sun, they travelled a short while toward the sun,
And left the vivid air signed with their honour.

Stephen Spender

Jan van Eyck, *Adoration of the Mystic Lamb, The Ghent Altarpiece*

The subject of the central panel of the altarpiece has often been interpreted as an All Saints' theme. The fifteenth-century artist placed the lamb, symbol of Christ, in the center of Christian history: pagan people living before the time of Christ, people from the Hebrew Scriptures, apostles and those who witnessed to their Christian faith, including those men and women who were martyred for their beliefs.

Yet, through me flashes
this vision of a magnetic field of the soul,
created in a timeless present by unknown multitudes,
living in holy obedience,
whose words and actions are a timeless prayer—
"The Communion of Saints"
  —and—within it—an eternal life.

Dag Hammarskjöld

Cappella della Velatio: Lunette with Orant, Catacomb of Priscilla, Rome

Early Christians had a profound sense of being linked through faith to those who had gone before them in death. Throughout the catacombs in which many early Christians were buried are found *Orants* (from the Latin *ora* to pray) like the woman pictured here, figures of dead persons presented as if alive, with hands upraised in the act of prayer. Christians living under persecution were comforted and reassured by these images of the dead—who God had already delivered —praying for *them* in their own times of trial.

Bridegroom of poverty, our brother
Francis, follower of Jesus and friend
of creation:
Stand here beside us.

Apostle of nonviolence, Gandhi the
Mahatma, reproach to the churches:
Stand here beside us.

John XXIII, Pope and friend of the poor,
who longed for the unity of all people:
Stand here beside us.

Peacemakers in the world,
Dag Hammarskjöld and Desmond Tutu,
called children of God:
Stand here beside us.

Mask of the Christ, Gautama the Buddha,
and Mother Teresa, fountains of compassion:
Stand here beside us.

Harriet Tubman and Frederick Douglass,
and all fighters for freedom:
Stand here beside us.

…

Students of the earth, Charles Darwin, Pierre
Teilhard de Chardin and Margaret Mead,
voyagers in the past and in the future:
Stand here beside us.

Children of the Synagogue, Albert Einstein,
Karl Marx, and Sigmund Freud, divers
in the sea of humanity:
Stand here beside us.

Confessors in chains, Dietrich Bonhoeffer,
and the Berrigan[s], war resisters:
Stand here beside us.

Confessor in Africa, Augustine of Hippo,
city-planner for God's people:
Stand here beside us.

Innocents of Wounded Knee and My Lai,
God's wheat ground in the mill of war:
Stand here beside us.

Martyrs of Africa, Perpetua, mother;
Felicity, slave; and all your companions:
Stand here beside us.

…

Martyr in Colombia, Camillo Torres,
priest and revolutionary:
Stand here beside us.

…

Unwed mother, Blessed Mary, fair well–
spring of our liberation:
Stand here beside us.

Our leader and Lord, Jesus the Son
of God, bright cornerstone of our unity
in a new Spirit:
Stand here beside us.

Almighty God, you have surrounded
us with a great cloud of witnesses:
Grant that we, encouraged by the good
example of these your servants, may
persevere in running the race that is set before
us, until at last, with all your saints attain
to your eternal joy: Through Jesus Christ,
the pioneer and perfecter of our faith,
who lives and reigns with you and the
Holy Spirit, one God, forever and ever.

Amen.

"Invocation of the Saints," in *The Covenant
of Peace—A Liberation Prayer Book*

Stand here beside us.

ZACCHAEUS, COME DOWN!

When Jesus came to the place, he looked and said to Zacchaeus, "Zacchaeus, hurry and come down; for I must stay at your house today." So Zacchaeus hurried down and was happy to welcome Jesus. All who saw it began to grumble and said, "He has gone to be the guest of one who is a sinner." Zacchaeus stood there and said to Jesus, "Look, half of my possessions I will give to the poor; and if I have defrauded anyone of anything, I will pay back four times as much."

Luke 19:5–8

Zacchaeus was
 A wee little man
 A wee little man was he
He climbed up in a sycamore tree
 For Jesus he wanted to see

Emil Nolde, *Hermit in Tree*

We wear the mask that grins and lies,
It hides our cheeks and shades our eyes—
This debt we pay to human guile;
With torn and bleeding hearts we smile,
And mouth with myriad subtleties.

Why should the world be overwise,
In counting all our tears and sighs?
Nay, let them only see us, while
     We wear the mask.

We smile, but, O great Christ, our cries
To thee from tortured souls arise.
We sing, but oh the clay is vile
Beneath our feet, and long the mile;
But let the world dream otherwise,
     We wear the mask!

Paul Laurence Dunbar

Zacchaeus' offer of half of his possessions to the poor and a generous restitution to anyone he may have cheated can be seen as itself evidence of the radicality of grace and the power of Jesus' good news to him. After all, Luke's gospel of grace is joined to repentance, and repentance is not solely a transaction of the heart. Repentance bears fruit.

Fred Craddock

Si fui motivo de dolor, oh Dios;
si por mi causa el débil tropezó;
si en tus caminos yo no quise andar,
¡perdón, oh Dios!

Si vana y fútil mi palabra fue;
si al que sufría en su dolor dejé;
no me condenes, tú, por mi maldad,
¡perdón, oh Dios!

Si por la vida quise andar en paz,
tranquilo, libre y sin luchar por ti
cuando anhelabas verme en la lid,
¡perdón, oh Dios!

Escucha oh Dios, mi humilde confesión
y líbrame de tentación sutil;
preserva siempre mi alma en tu redil.
Amén, Amén.

If I have been the source of pain, O God;
If to the weak I have refused my strength;
If, in rebellion, I have strayed away;
Forgive me, God.

If I have spoken words of cruelty;
If I have left some suffering unrelieved;
Condemn not my insensitivity;
Forgive me, God.

If I've insisted on a peaceful life,
Far from the struggles that the gospel brings,
When you prefer to guide me to the strife,
Forgive me, God.

Receive, O God, this ardent word of prayer,
And free me from temptation's subtle snare,
With tender patience, lead me to your care.
Amen, Amen.

Sara M. de Hall, based on a text by C. M. Battersby,
translated by Janet M. May

There was a man in Jericho called Zacchaeus.
There was a man in Jericho called Zacchaeus.
Now the Hebrews they were tall,
But Zacchaeus he was small,
   Yet the Lord loved Zacchaeus better than them all.

   The Lord went walking one day through Jericho Town
And the people began to gather from miles around.
But Zacchaeus he couldn't see,
So he climbed a sycamore tree,
And the Lord looked up and said, "Zacchaeus come down."

   ...

Now Zacchaeus was small of stature,
But he could show
That a man who is stout of heart can grow and grow

   ...

And salvation came that day to his whole household.

Miriam Therese Winter

ETERNAL COMFORT, GOOD HOPE

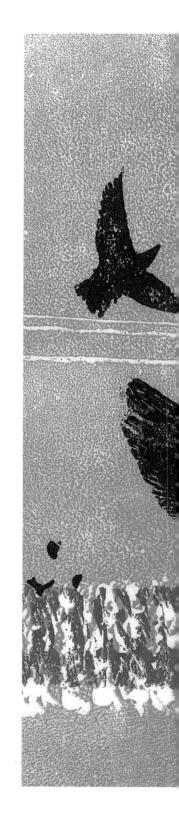

Now may our Lord Jesus Christ himself and God our Parent, who loved us and through grace gave us eternal comfort and good hope, comfort your hearts and strengthen them in every good work and word.

2 Thessalonians 2:16–17

Be Like the Bird

Be like the bird, who

Halting in his flight

On limb too slight

Feels it give way beneath him,

Yet sings

Knowing he hath wings.

Victor Hugo

Walter Williams, *Caged Bird*

Ellis Wilson, *Funeral Procession*

The noun and the verb *comfort* translate a Greek word that means literally "called alongside."

Jesus and God are "alongside" us to give us strength; and the word comfort with its Latin roots means literally "with strength."

Comfort is more than a pat on the back. It is Jesus' and God's presence to strengthen us in the present and give us good hope for an eternal future.

Paul Hammer

to **give** *us* **strength**

On the rough wet grass
of the back yard my
father and mother have
spread quilts. . . .
The stars are wide and
alive, they seem each like
a smile of great sweetness
and they seem very near.
All my people are larger
bodies than mine, quiet,
with voices gentle and
meaningless like the
voices of sleeping birds. . . .
By some chance we are
all here on this earth; and
who shall ever tell the
sorrow of being on this earth,
lying, on quilts, on the grass,
in a summer evening,
among the sounds of the night.
May God bless my people,
my uncle, my aunt, my mother,
my good father, oh, remember
them kindly in their time
of trouble; and in the hour
of their taking away.

After a little I am taken
in and put to bed. Sleep, soft
smiling, draws me unto her:
and those receive me,
who quietly treat me, as one
familiar and well-beloved
in that home.

James Agee

BY YOUR ENDURANCE

They asked Jesus, "Teacher, when will this be?" And Jesus said, "Beware that you are not led astray; for many will come in my name and say 'I am the one!' and 'The time is near!' Do not go after them. You will be hated by all because of my name. But not a hair of your head will perish. By your endurance you will gain your lives."

Luke 21:7a, 8, 17–19

The end is not yet. During the time of testimony, disciples will experience suffering. They are not exempt. There is nothing here of . . . an arrogance born of a doctrine of a rapture in which believers are removed from the scenes of persecution and suffering. There are no scenes here of cars crashing into one another on the highways because their drivers have been blissfully raptured. The word of Jesus in our lesson is still forceful: "This will give you an opportunity to testify. . . . By your endurance you will gain your souls."

Fred Craddock

Rembrandt Harmensz van Rijn, *Two Women Teaching a Child to Walk*

Sing, pray and swerve not from God's ways,

But do thine own part faithfully;

Trust the rich promises of grace,

so shall they be fulfilled in thee.

God never yet forsook at need

The soul secured by trust indeed.

Georg Neumark

In your patience you will gain your souls.

Luke 21:19, Danish Bible, 1830

Noel Counihan,
Homage to Goya (Requiem for El Salvador)

This painting represents
both the artist's tribute to those
in Latin America engaged
in the struggle against oppression
and his protest against all injustice.
Both the figure and the title
of the work refer to Goya's painting
The Third of May, 1808,
which depicted an instance of massive
injustice in Spanish history.

Rosemary Crumlin

Since it is by God's mercy that we are engaged in this ministry, we do not lose heart. . . . We are afflicted in every way, but not crushed; perplexed, but not driven to despair; persecuted, but not forsaken; struck down, but not destroyed; always carrying in the body the death of Jesus, so that the life of Jesus may also be made visible in our bodies.

2 Corinthians 4:1, 8–10

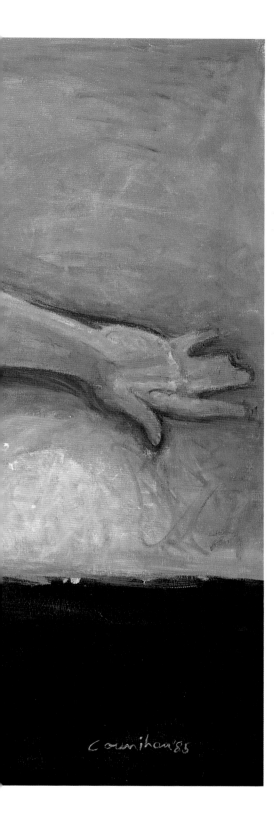

When the thunder rumbles

Now the Age of Gold is dead

And the dreams we've clung to dying to stay young

Have left us parched and old instead. . . .

When my spirit falters on decaying altars

And my illusions fail,

I go on right then.

I go on again.

I go on to say

I will celebrate another day. . . .

I go on. . . .

If tomorrow tumbles

And everything I love is gone

I will face regret

All my days, and yet

I will still go on . . . on . . .

Lauda, Lauda, Laude

Lauda, Lauda di da di day . . .

Leonard Bernstein, Stephen Schwarz

Done made my vow to the Lord,

And I never will turn back,

Oh I will go, I shall go

To see what the end will be.

Sometimes I'm up, sometimes I'm down

(see what the end will be),

But still my soul is heav'nly bound

(see what the end will be).

When I was a mourner, just like you

(see what the end will be),

I prayed and prayed 'til I came through

(see what the end will be).

Traditional Spiritual

GOD REMEMBERS

T hen the child's father Zechariah was filled with the Holy Spirit and spoke this prophecy: "Blessed be the Lord God of Israel, for God has looked favorably on God's people and redeemed them. God has shown the mercy promised to our ancestors, and has remembered God's holy covenant."

Luke 1:67–68, 72

My bow I set in the clouds to be a sign of the covenant between myself and the earth. When I bring clouds over the earth, the rainbow will appear in the clouds.

Genesis 9:13–14

Alma Thomas, *The Eclipse*

Refusing to conform to established styles,
the artist has created her own way of seeing.
Her whirl of colors evokes the rainbow,
the sign of God's covenant.

And you whose spirit is sad and unsure, try to remember
    the very best parts of your life, the loveliest
    feelings in your body self,
    occasions of bold delight and quiet confidence,
moments of unambivalent commitment and unrestrained joy.
Try to remember when you have believed passionately in
    something or someone human or divine.
Try to imagine that someone now believes in you
    because she trusts your loveliest feelings
    . . . commitments. . . confidence. . . joy.
She goes with us as we are called forth to go, with one
    another, evoked by historical memory
    and voices audible only to ears that can hear the
    power of God in history.
Her name is love.

Carter Heyward

Edward Larson (design), Verla Shilling (quilter), *Missouri Farm, Newton County*

Quilting is memory's art. New fabrics combine with old skills to create a vision of the past in all its color, complexity, and texture.

PRAYER OF CONFESSION

You must be able to think back to streets in unknown neighborhoods, to unexpected encounters, and to partings you had long seen coming; to days of childhood whose mystery is still unexplained, to parents whom you had to hurt when they brought you a toy and you didn't pick it up. . . . You must have memories of many nights of love, each one different from all the others, memories of women screaming in labor, and of light, pale, sleeping girls who have given birth and are closing again. . . . And it is not yet enough to have memories. . . . Only when they have changed into our very blood, into glances and gestures, and are nameless, no longer to be distinguished from ourselves—only then can it happen that in some very rare hour the first word of a poem arises in their midst and goes forth from them.

Malte Laurids Brigge

Almighty God,
I come to you
because I am struggling inside.
I dwell on past hurts and heartaches
and refuse to let them go and forgive.
For that, forgive me.
I spend so much time as a worrier,
looking within,
that I forget the promise of your [child],
given for me.
For that I need forgiveness.
I focus too many times on useless speculation of the unknown
and fail to recall your promise
of the Holy Spirit.
Forgive me!
For not remembering that you . . .
live within and beside me
Forever.
Amen.

International Fellowship of Metropolitan
Community Church, Key West

For God to act with mercy in Jesus was to remember, that is, to "make present."

Paul Hammer

Advent

D. A. Siqueiros, *Peasant Mother*, detail

"In my beginning is my end," asserts T. S. Eliot in *Four Quartets*. Much of what we believe about God and Christ is reflected therein: the God who made us will be the God who judges us; Christ is the Alpha and the Omega; the God who created the world out of nothing will at its consummation be "all in all."

So with ritual cycles. We begin them where we end. The Advent season begins the liturgical year and the lectionary cycle with stories about the end time: "Stay awake!" "Live in expectation!" "Watch for signs of the reign of God!" But in our end is our beginning: the signs of God's reign point us to the birth of something new.

The colors for Advent are purple or deep blue. For some, the blue reflects the color of late autumn's night, a sky lit by moon and stars. The days are short. The long nights mark the end of the year's growing season. But the long nights are fertile ground for dreaming— imagine the desert blossoming and sheltering a mother and child; imagine peace prevailing; imagine God all in all. Joseph dreams in this season—of the child to be born soon, whom he is to name Emmanuel, God-with-us.

Advent: watch and wait; imagine and dream. The signs of the season are all around, pointing us to our beginning and our end. God with us!

LIVE IN EXPECTATION

LIVE IN EXPECTATION

Keep awake therefore, for you do not know on what day your Lord is coming. But understand this: if the owner of the house had known in what part of the night the thief was coming, the owner would have stayed awake and would not have let the house be broken into. Therefore you also must be ready, for God's future Ruler and Judge is coming at an unexpected hour.

Matthew 24:42–44

"Sleepers, wake!" A voice astounds us;
The shout of rampart guards surrounds us:
"Awake, Jerusalem, arise!"
Midnight's peace their cry has broken,
Their urgent summons clearly spoken:
"The time has come, O maidens wise!
Rise up, and give us light;
The Bridegroom is in sight.
Alleluia! Your lamps prepare and hasten there,
That you the wedding feast may share."

Philipp Nicolai and Carl P. Daw, Jr.

Cross of the Community, artisans of La Palma, El Salvador

This cross and others like it have been produced in El Salvador since the latter years of the civil war there. The crosses are remarkable for their use of color and images of hope in a situation of despair. The woman's figure at the center of the cross with her arms spread wide at once suggests the form of the crucified Jesus and the triumphant risen Christ who is embodied in the works of hope of the Salvadoran people, going about the ordinary business of life —teaching, healing, farming—in the extraordinary time of war.

Toda la Tierra (All Earth Is Waiting)

Toda la tierra espera al Salvador
y el surco abierto,
la obra del Creador;
es el mundo que lucha por la libertad,
reclama justicia y busca la verdad.

All earth is waiting to see the Promised One,
and open furrows, the sowing of our God.
All the world, bound and struggling, seeks true liberty;
it cries out for justice and searches for the truth.

Mountains and valleys will have to be made plain;
open new highways, new highways for our God,
Who is now coming closer, so come all and see,
and open the doorways as wide as wide can be.

Alberto Taulè, translated by Gertrude C. Suppe

Leader: O Wisdom, who proceeds from the mouth of the Most High, reaching from beginning to end, mightily and sweetly ordering all things:

All: *Come and teach us the way of prudence. . . .*

Leader: O Root of Jesse, emblem of the people, before whom kings keep silent, to whom nations pray:

All: *Come deliver us. Do not delay!*

Leader: O Rising Sun, Splendor of eternal Light and Sun of Justice:

All: *Come and enlighten those who sit in darkness and in the shadow of death.*

Leader: O Ruler of nations, the Desired of all, the Cornerstone that unites:

All: *Come and save the people you created out of clay.*

Leader: O Emmanuel, our Ruler and Lawgiver, the Expectation and Savior of the nations:

All: *Come and save us, O God.*

Leader: Let us pray.
O Child of God, our Savior,
today we await your coming,
and tomorrow we shall see your glory.
Reveal the good news to all of us
who long for your arrival.
Come, Love incarnate, do not delay.
Come, Lord Jesus! Amen.

Miriam Therese Winter

Keep awake

therefore, for you do not know on what day your Lord is coming!

Glen Strock, *Rapture at Rio Arriba*

Rapture at Rio Arriba whimsically depicts the suddenness of the end time. The "unexpected hour" of God's future reign has broken in on the community of Rio Arriba, and they are lifted out of their ordinary lives.

Advent's theme of expectation points us forward not only to the incarnation of Jesus, celebrated at Christmas, but also to the awaited final coming of Christ, when God's Dominion will break in on us and God will be "all in all."

A DREAM OF PEACE

the wolf shall live with the lamb,

the leopard shall lie down with the kid,

the calf and the lion and the fatling

together, and a little child shall lead

them. The nursing child shall play

over the hole of the asp, and the weaned

child shall put its hands on the adder's

den. They will not hurt or destroy on

all my holy mountain; for the earth will

be full of the knowledge of God as the

waters cover the sea.

Isaiah 11:6, 8–9

A shoot shall come out from
    the stump of Jesse,
and a branch shall grow out of
    his roots.
The spirit of God shall rest
    on him,
the spirit of wisdom and
    understanding,
the spirit of counsel and might,
the spirit of knowledge and fear of God.

Isaiah 11:1–2

C. Terry Saul, *Tree of Jesse*

C. Terry Saul paints the ancient Hebrew prophecy of Isaiah from his Chickasaw/Choctaw worldview.
The Promised One is born of the Spirit, cradled in the arms of Mary, nurtured by branch after branch,
by elder after elder that preceded him. The tree of Jesse leads to Isaiah's vision of peace within all of creation.

Root of Jesse

Root of Jesse
rising
from many an ancient prophecy

promised child
to all who would be reconciled
breaks through at last.

A virgin shoot accepts
God's seed
bows to the Mighty Deed.
One branch
bears bud, flower, fruit:
Christ blossoms as David's root.

Lord, you are stem, stalk, tree!
Let your fruit take root in me.

Miriam Therese Winter

John August Swanson, *Peaceable Kingdom*

no more wars,

Peace unto you. Shalom, salaam, forever.

God, you shape our dreams.
As we put our trust in you
may your hopes and desires
be ours,
and we your expectant people.
Amen.

A New Zealand Prayer Book

THE DESERT BLOSSOMS

The wilderness and the dry land

shall be glad, the desert shall rejoice

and blossom; like the crocus

it shall blossom abundantly.

Say to those who are of a fearful

heart, "Be strong, do not fear!

Here is your God. God will come

with vengeance, with terrible

recompense. God will come

and save you."

Isaiah 35:1–2a, 4

William James Warren, *Deserts: Dry Lake Bed*

Joy Shall Come

Joy shall come even to the wilderness,
    And the parched land shall then know great gladness;
As the rose, as the rose shall deserts blossom,
    Deserts like a garden blossom.
For the living springs shall give cool water,
    In the desert streams shall flow,
For living springs shall give cool water,
    In the desert streams shall flow.

Hebrew Traditional

D. A. Siqueiros, *Peasant Mother*

The desert will sing and rejoice
and the wilderness will blossom with flowers;
and will see the Lord's splendor,
see the Lord's greatness and power.
Tell everyone who is anxious:
Be strong and don't be afraid.
The blind will be able to see;
the deaf will be able to hear;
the lame will leap and dance;
those who can't speak will shout.
They will hammer their swords into ploughs
and their spears into pruning-knives;
the nations will live in peace;
they will train for war no more.
This is the promise of God;
God's promise will be fulfilled.

Iona Community Worship Book

blessed be you, harsh matter, barren soil, stubborn rock:
you who yield only to force, you who cause us to work
if we would eat.

Blessed be you, perilous matter, violent sea, untamable passion:
you who, unless we fetter you, will devour us.

Blessed be you, mighty matter, irresistible march of evolution,
reality ever new-born; you who, by constantly shattering
our mental categories, force us to go ever further and further
in our pursuit of the truth.

Blessed be you, universal matter, immeasurable time,
boundless ether, triple abyss of stars and atoms and generations:
you who by overflowing and dissolving our narrow standards
or measurements reveal to us the dimensions of God.

Blessed be you, impenetrable matter: you who, interposed
between our minds and the world of essences, cause us to languish
with the desire to pierce through the seamless veil of phenomena.

Blessed be you, mortal matter: you who one day will undergo
the process of dissolution within us and will thereby take us
forcibly into the very heart of that which exists.

. . .

You who batter us and then dress our wounds,
you who resist and yield to us,
you who wreck and build,
you who shackle and liberate,
the sap of our souls,
the hand of God,
the flesh of Christ:
it is you, matter, that I bless.

Pierre Teilhard de Chardin

Mark Harris, *Oakland Fire*

i thank You God for most this amazing day
for the leaping greenly spirits of trees
and a blue true dream of sky; and for everything
which is natural which is infinite which is yes

(i who have died am alive again today,
and this is the sun's birthday; this is the birth
day of life and of love and wings: and of the gay
great happening illimitably earth)

how should tasting touching hearing seeing
breathing any—lifted from the no
of all nothing—human merely being
doubt unimaginable you?

(now the ears of my ears awake and
now the eyes of my eyes are opened)

E. E. Cummings

The desert will sing and rejoice...

NAME THE CHILD EMMANUEL

She will bear a son, and you are to name him Jesus, for Jesus will save the people from their sins. All this took place to fulfill what had been spoken by God through the prophet: "Look, the virgin shall conceive and bear a son, and they shall name him Emmanuel," which means, "God is with us."

Matthew 1:21–23

Toda la Tierra (All Earth Is Waiting)

Dice el profeta al pueblo de Israel:
"De madre virgen ya viene Emmanuel,"
será "Dios con nosotros," hermano será,
con él la esperanza al mundo volverá.

Thus says the prophet to those of Israel,
"A virgin mother will bear Emmanuel":
One whose name is "God with us," our Savior shall be,
through whom hope will blossom once more within our hearts.

Alberto Taulé, translated by Gertrude C. Suppe

William Ebbets, *Oswaldo Chin, Beekeeper, and Manuel* (opposite)

The traditional image of Joseph is of an old man, although nothing in the Scriptures supports this. The "dreamer" of Matthew's first chapters may well have been as young, and ordinary, and beautiful as the father of this "Manuel."

WHAT you gonna name THAT pretty Little Baby?

Oh, Mary, what you gonna name that pretty little Baby? Glory, Glory to the new born King! Some will call Him one thing, but I think I'll call Him Jesus! Glory, Glory, Glory, Glory to the new born King!

The Name Cuts Deep

Here's another one.
A boy, eight days old.
It's time: time to cut away
Unneeded flesh, to sign the scar
Of God in manchild's private place.
No one else will know but him and his.

The rite calls for a name.
Have you a name yet, son?
What shall we call you, little giant?
Call his name "Jesus"? Why?
Because he'll save his people?
What a huge load for such little shoulders.
What dreams parents have, what expectancies.
Poor little child, to have God's work
Assigned so soon.

Cut the name in deep. Tattoo it indelibly on tortured Hebrew flesh.
Scar it with raw wounds to acquaint you early
With cross and barbs and nail.
You'll be Jew soon enough to know
The Name cuts deep in certain flesh.
Now you belong to God.
There's no escaping that.
His name for eternity. Get used to it now.
"Jesus" is the handle you'll get used by.
You'll wish you could change your name
Into incognito, when the whole world
Calls it out in curse and prayer.

Go home for now, lacerated boy.
Don't grow up too soon.

Wayne Saffen

Aminah Brenda Lynn Robinson,
What You Gonna Name That Pretty Little Baby? (opposite)

After eight days had passed,

it was time to circumcise

the child; and he was called Jesus,

the name given by the angel

before he was conceived in the womb.

Luke 2:21

We are called to proclaim the truth. . . . And let us believe:
It is not true that this world and its people are
doomed to die and to be lost.
This is true: I have come that they may have life
in all its abundance.

It is not true that we must accept inhumanity and
discrimination, hunger and poverty, death and destruction.
This is true: the deaf hear, the dead are raised to life,
the poor are hearing the good news.

It is not true that violence and hatred should have the last
word, and that war and destruction have come to stay forever.
This is true: death shall be no more, neither shall there
be mourning nor crying nor pain anymore.

It is not true that we are simply victims of the powers of
evil who seek to rule the world.
This is true: the Lord whom we seek will suddenly
come to the temple; and the Lord is like a refiner's fire.

It is not true that our dreams of liberation, of human dignity,
are not meant for this earth and for this history.
This is true: it is already time for us to wake from sleep.
For the night is far gone, the day is at hand.

Allan Boesak

Christmas

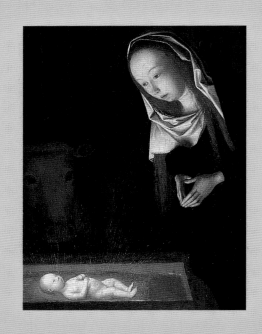

Geertgen tot Sint Jans,
The Nativity, at Night, detail

Jesus is born, Sun of Righteousness,

and the world is illumined by new light.

Jesus is born, Sun of Righteousness, and the world is illumined by new light. As the light emanating from the manger in Geertgen tot Sint Jans's *The Nativity, at Night* illuminates all the faces of those present at the birth, so too we, in light of Jesus incarnate, see our world and our relationships anew.

The light from the manger reveals that the dream vision has become a reality: new relationships are possible, relationships characterized by the righteousness, wisdom, and peace Jesus comes to bring. All our expectations of power are upset. God's grandeur is revealed in the manger, the power of God manifest in a homeless child. The ruler of peace, God's word of wisdom, has been made flesh, hope incarnate—Jesus Christ lives, moves, and has being in this world and the world lives, moves, and has being in Christ—nothing will be the same again. Christ in intimate relationship with us will show us the way to fullness of life: justice, peace, the reign of God! "Born in the night, Mary's child . . ."

Creation responds: "Gloria!" All creatures—from angels on high to sea creatures from the depths!

And the church celebrates in its white robes—"Gloria!" for twelve days, reveling in the joy of the Word among us.

REVELING IN THE JOY OF GOD AMONG US

All things were made through the Word, and without the Word was not anything made that was made. In the Word was life, and the life was the light of all. The light shines in the deepest night, and the night has not overcome it.

John 1:3–5

Candlelight Carol

How do you capture the wind on the water?
How do you count all the stars in the sky?
How can you measure the love of a mother?
Or how can you write down a baby's first cry?

…

Find him at Bethlehem laid in a manger:
Christ our Redeemer asleep in the hay.
Godhead incarnate and hope of salvation:
A child with his mother that first Christmas Day.

Candlelight, angel light, firelight and starglow
Shine on his cradle till breaking of dawn.
Gloria, gloria in excelsis Deo!
Angels are singing; the Christ child is born.

John Rutter

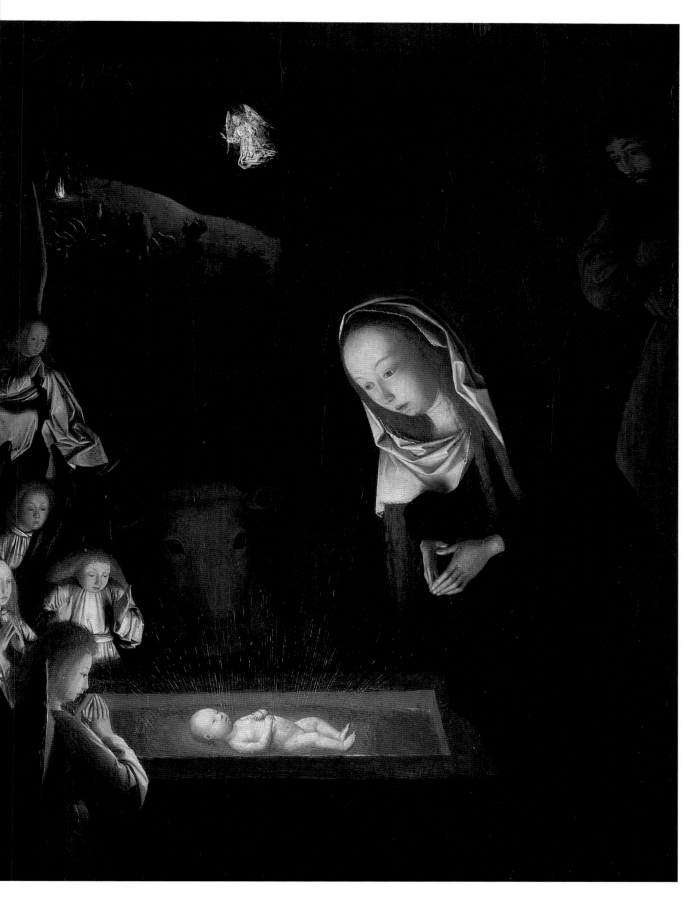

Shine on

his cradle till

breaking of dawn.

John Rutter

Geertgen tot Sint Jans,
The Nativity, at Night

Light from Jesus in the manger
illumines all who are present—
human, animal, and angel.

Virgin and Child, Coptic personal icon

As we are glad, Creator God,

when the dawn reveals the world to us,

innocent and fresh,

so we may discover the infant in the manger,

and in delight be ready to start anew.

New Zealand Prayer Book

BORN IN THE NIGHT, MARY'S CHILD

Born in the night, Mary's Child, a long way from Your home;
Coming in need, Mary's Child, born in a borrowed room.

Clear shining light, Mary's Child, Your face lights up our way;
Light of the world, Mary's Child, dawn on our darkened day.

Truth of our life, Mary's Child, You tell us God is good;
Yes, it is true, Mary's Child, dawn on our darkened day.

Truth of our life, Mary's Child, You tell us God is good;
Yes, it is true, Mary's Child, shown on your cross of wood.

Hope of the world, Mary's Child, You're coming soon to reign;
King of the earth, Mary's Child, walk in our streets again.

Geoffrey Ainger

P

raise God! Praise God from the heavens;

praise God in the heights! Praise God,

all God's angels; praise God, all God's host!

Praise God from the earth, you water

spouts and ocean depths; young men and

women alike, old and young together!

Let them praise the name of God for God's

name alone is exalted!

Psalm 148:1–2, 7, 12–13a

Toda la Tierra

All Earth Is Waiting

En un pesebre
Jesús apareció,
pero en el mundo está
presente hoy.

*In lowly stable
the Promised One appeared,
yet feel that presence
throughout the earth today.*

Alberto Taulè,
translated by Gertrude C. Suppe

Mark Wyland, *Whaling Wall VI: Hawaiian Humpbacks*

At the birth of the Christ, all heaven and earth rejoiced. In Matthew the sparkling star becomes the Messiah's star. In Luke the angels declare to the shepherds the good news of Jesus' birth to all creation. "Peace on earth . . ."

103

GOD IN THE FLESH

And the Word became flesh

and dwelt among us,

full of grace and truth.

John 1:14a

**You have come
to us as a small child,
but you have
brought us the greatest
of all gifts, the gift
of eternal love.
Caress us with your
tiny hands, embrace us
with your tiny arms,
and pierce our hearts with
your soft, sweet cries.**

Bernard of Clairvaux, 1090–1153

Cribb'd, cabined, and confined within the contours of a human infant. The infinite defined by the finite? The Creator of all life thirsty and abandoned? Why would [God] do such a thing? Aren't there easier ways for God to redeem . . . fallen creatures?

Madeleine L'Engle

Emil Nolde, *Holy Night* (opposite)

*Emerging from
the granite prison
is a human being,
taking shape
before our eyes.
The struggle to burst
forth — stone becoming
human form —
stirs us to imagine
God's Word
becoming flesh.*

Michelangelo, *Awakening Prisoner*

"And the Word *became flesh*" is a christological affirmation of a radical nature with far-reaching implications for our thinking about God, life in the world, and what it means to be Christian. Analogies about changing clothes, as in the stories of a [ruler] who wears peasant clothing in order to move among his subjects freely, are not adequate for clarifying John 1:14. The church has always had members who wanted to protect their Christ from John 1:14 with phrases such as "seemed to be," "appeared," and "in many ways was like" flesh. Whatever else John 1:14 means, it does state without question the depth, the intensity, and the pursuit of God's love for the world.

Fred B. Craddock

. . . the **disguise** of the **divine**

Those Who Saw the Star

The Word, for our sake, became poverty clothed as the poor who
live off the refuse heap.

The Word, for our sake, became agony in the shrunken breast
of the woman grown old by the absence of her murdered husband.

The Word, for our sake, became a sob a thousand times stifled
in the immovable mouth of the child who died from hunger. . . .

The Word became an ever-present absence among the 70,000
families torn apart by death. . . .

The *word-knife* cut us deeply in that place of shame:
the painful reality of the poor.

The Word blew its spirit over the dried bones of the
Mummified-Churches, guardians of silence.

The Word, that *early-morning-bugle*, awoke us from the lethargy
which had robbed us of our Hope.

The Word became a path in the jungle, a decision on the farm,
love in women, unity among workers,
and a Star for those few who can inspire dreams.

The Word became Light,
The Word became History,
The Word became Conflict,
The Word became Indomitable Spirit,
and sowed its seeds. . . .

and *those-of-good-will* heard the angels sing . . . .

The Word became flesh in a *nation-pregnant-with-freedom*,
The Spirit strengthened the arms which forged Hope,
The Verb became flesh in the people who perceived a new day. . . .
The Word became the *seed-of-justice*,
and we conceived *peace* . . . .

Julia Esquivel

Rejoice over everything.
Exult. Exhilarate.
Be glad. Be delighted, elated,
and bowled over with joy!
Frolic freely, hop, hope,
dance on the dare, cheer,
champion the little ones,
revel in the riotous light.
Invoke God without ceasing.
Pray with passion.
Whatever you do,
do not quench the Spirit.
Take care not to douse
or dampen the bold blaze
in your depths.
Jump into life.
Hold fast to it.
Give thanks for everything.
For everything,
even the most misshapen
and misunderstood,
is the disguise of the divine.

Susan Virginia Hull

Peter Paul Rubens
Christ

107

Epiphany

James Jacques Joseph Tissot, *Journey of the Magi*, detail

The revelation of God in Christ is clear:

"This is my Child, my Beloved,

with whom I am well pleased."

Epiphany is the season that makes Jesus' identity manifest. The Christ, the anointed of God, is revealed to the whole world, made present symbolically in the persons of the Magi. These sojourners from the East seek, recognize, and adore the child Jesus as the Christ.

Traditionally the season of Epiphany starts with the story of the Magi. It continues in the weeks before Lent with the stories of Jesus' baptism in the Jordan and the first of his signs at the wedding of Cana. It concludes with the account of his transfiguration before the closest of his disciples. For those who have eyes to see and ears to hear, the revelation of God in Christ is clear: "This is my child, my Beloved, with whom I am well pleased."

The season of Epiphany explores our identities as well: we are those who, like the Magi, seek. John the Baptist poses the question that defines us: "What are you seeking?"

We seek the revelation of God in the person of Jesus the Christ—to know and love and follow him.

The season is framed in celebratory white at the festivals of Epiphany, the Baptism of Jesus, and the Transfiguration. But for our seeking in between those festivals we wear the green of ordinary time.

WHO IS THIS JESUS?

JOURNEY OF THE MAGI

When they saw the star, they rejoiced exceedingly with great joy; and going into the house they saw the child with Mary his mother, and they fell down and worshiped him. Then, opening their treasures, they offered the child gifts, gold and frankincense and myrrh.

Matthew 2:10–11

James Jacques Joseph Tissot, *Journey of the Magi*

Journey of the Magi

This imaginative reflection on the magi is not too far from Matthew's own intent. In the persons of the magi Matthew was anticipating the Gentile Christians of his own community. Although these had as their birthright only the revelation of God in nature, they had been attracted to Jesus; and when instructed in the Scriptures of the Jews, they had come to believe in and pay homage to the Messiah.

Raymond E. Brown

A cold coming we had of it,
Just the worst time of the year
For a journey, and such a long journey:
The ways deep and the weather sharp,
The very dead of winter.
And the camels galled, sore-footed, refractory
Lying down in the melting snow.
There were times we regretted
The summer palaces on slopes, the terraces,
And the silken girls bringing sherbet.
Then the camel men cursing and grumbling
And running away, and wanting their liquor and women,
And the night-fires going out, and the lack of shelters,
And the cities hostile and the towns unfriendly
And the villages dirty and charging high prices:
A hard time we had of it.
At the end we preferred to travel all night,
Sleeping in snatches,
With the voices singing in our ears, saying
That this was all folly.

Then at dawn we came down to a temperate valley,
Wet, below the snow line, smelling of vegetation;
With a running stream and a water-mill beating the darkness,
And three trees on the low sky,
And an old white horse galloped away in the meadow.
Then we came to a tavern with vine-leaves over the lintel,
Six hands at an open door dicing for pieces of silver,
And feet kicking the empty wine-skins.
But there was no information, and so we continued
And arrived at evening, not a moment too soon
Finding the place; it was (you may say) satisfactory.

All this was a long time ago, I remember,
And I would do it again, but set down
This set down
This: Were we led all that way for
Birth or Death? There was a Birth, certainly,
We had evidence and no doubt. I had seen birth and death,
But had thought they were different; this Birth was
Hard and bitter agony for us, like Death, our death.
We returned to our places, these Kingdoms,
But no longer at ease here, in the old dispensation,
With an alien people clutching their god.
I should be glad of another death.

T. S. Eliot

At the sound of the knock, Amahl's mother awoke with a start but didn't move from her bed on the bench. "Amahl," she said drowsily, "go and see who's knocking at the door."

"Yes, Mother." He went to the door and opened it a crack, his heart thudding in his chest. He closed the door quickly and rushed to his mother.

Amahl was shaking with excitement. "Mother—" he stopped. He hardly dared telll her what he had seen. "Outside the door there is"—he swallowed and went on with an effort—"there is a king with a crown."

She went with determination toward the door and Amahl limped close behind her. As the door swung open and she saw the three kings standing there in all their splendor, she caught her breath. She bowed to them in utter amazement.

"Good evening," said the tall king with sweet blue eyes and a long white beard. "I am King Melchior." He wore rich robes trimmed with ermine, and silver slippers, and his voice was majestic but very kindly.

"Good evening," said a black king softly. "I am King Balthazar." He, too, was tall, but dark-bearded, and he wore robes of gold and scarlet and leopard skin.

"Good evening," said the third king. "I am Kaspar."

Amahl wanted to laugh with delight. Kaspar's robes, while they were rich, didn't fit him very well, and his crown was askew on his head as if he had just slapped it on any old way. His shoes didn't match either— one was gold and the other was purple. Amahl whispered triumphantly to his mother, "What did I tell you?"

"Noble sires," she said in an awed voice.

The black king, Balthazar, asked gently, "May we rest a while in your house and warm ourselves by your fireplace?"

Amahl's mother answered humbly, "I am a poor widow. A cold fireplace and a bed of straw are all I have to offer you. To these you are welcome."

King Kaspar, who seemed to be a little deaf, cupped his ear. "What did she say?" Balthazar answered him. "That we are welcome."

Kaspar smiled down at Amahl and his mother. Amahl clapped his hands with excitement. "Oh, thank you, thank you, thank you!" exclaimed Kaspar.

Then the three kings said together, "Thank you!"

Gian-Carlo Menotti

Light of the world,
we bow before You
in awe and adoration.
Bless us
and our simple faith
seeking understanding.
Epiphany means
manifestation,
lifting the veil,
revelation.
Reveal to us then
what we need to know
to love You,
and serve You,
and keep Your word
with fidelity and truth,
courage and hope,
this day and always.
Amen.

Miriam Therese Winter

Adoration of the Magi, detail of tomb, Cologne, Germany

t hen Peter began to speak to them:

"I truly understand that God shows

no partiality, but in every nation

anyone who fears God and does what

is right is acceptable to God.

You know the message God sent

to the people of Israel, preaching peace

by Jesus Christ—Christ is Lord of all."

Acts 10:34–36

BEATITUDES FOR FRIENDS AND FAMILY

Blessed are you who take time to listen
to difficult speech,
for you help us persevere until we are
understood.

Blessed are you who walk with us in public
places and ignore the stares of others,
for we find havens of relaxation in your
companionship.

Blessed are you who never bid us
to "hurry up," and more blessed
are you who do not snatch our
tasks from our hands to do them for us,
for often we need time—rather than help.

Blessed are you who stand beside us as
we enter new and untried ventures,
for the delight we feel when we surprise
you outweighs all the frustrating failures.

Blessed are you who ask for our help,
for our greatest need is to be needed.

Author Unknown

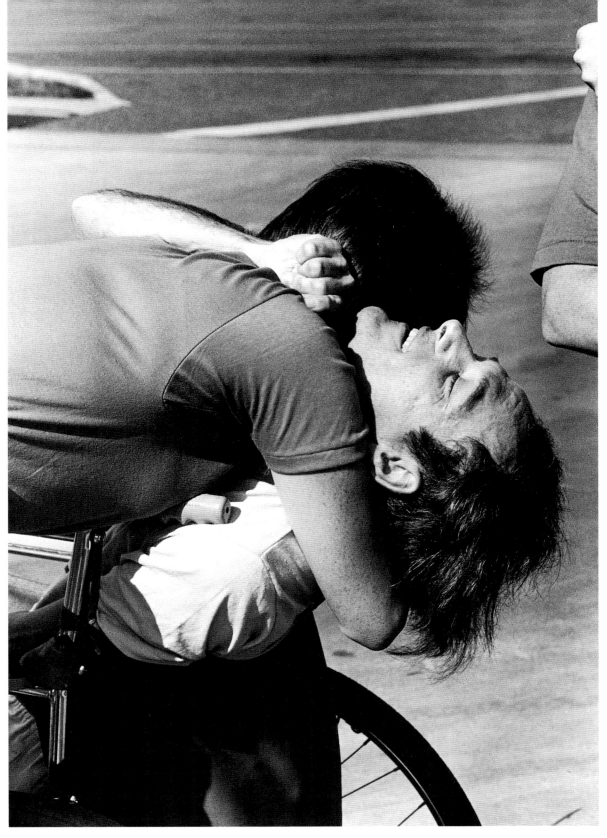

Elain Christensen, *Paul Remy, Camp Jabberwocky*, 1985

Camp Jabberwocky, on Martha's Vineyard, brings together both those with cerebral palsy and those who are able-bodied for an experience of community life.

Baptism of Legionnaire Cornelius by St. Peter

Cornelius was ripe for the church, and prayed constantly. Cornelius was ready for salvation. And that God should choose such a Gentile—a Roman, a soldier, an officer of centurion rank—is regarded as in itself sufficient to convince Peter and the church at Jerusalem—indeed, Judaism and the whole church of Luke's time—that "everyone who believes in [Jesus] receives forgiveness of sins through his name."

Fred D. Gealy

Almighty God,
as your Son our Savior
was born of a Hebrew mother,
but rejoiced in the faith of a Syrian woman
and of a Roman soldier,
welcomed the Greeks who sought him,
and suffered a man from Africa to carry his cross;
so teach us to regard [all faithful people]
as fellow heirs of the kingdom of Jesus Christ. . . .
Amen.

Toc H

Elain Christensen, *Paul Remy,*
Camp Jabberwocky, 1985, detail

Charles Schulz, *The Gospel According to Peanuts*

Hear Our Voices

Hear our voices, hear our song.

We will sing till all belong—

songs of welcome, midst the strife.

We hear music of new life.

Rick Yramategui

WHAT ARE YOU SEEKING?

The next day John again was standing with two of his disciples, and as he watched Jesus walk by, he exclaimed, "Look, here is the Lamb of God!" The two disciples heard him say this, and they followed Jesus. When Jesus turned and saw them following, he said to them, "What are you looking for?"

John 1:35–38a

Lamb of God
Bringer of Peace

Ethan Hubbard, *Young Herdsman, Peru*

Little Lamb, who made thee?
     Dost thou know who made thee?
Gave thee life and bid thee feed,
By the stream & o'er the mead;
Gave thee clothing of delight,
Softest clothing wooly bright;
Gave thee such a tender voice,
Making all the vales rejoice!
     Little Lamb who made thee?
     Dost thou know who made thee?

     Little Lamb I'll tell thee,
     Little Lamb I'll tell thee!
He is callèd by thy name,
For he calls himself a Lamb:
He is meek & he is mild,
He became a little child:
I a child & thou a lamb,
We are callèd by his name.
     Little Lamb God bless thee.
     Little Lamb God bless thee.

William Blake

Jan van Eyck, *Adoration of the Mystic Lamb*, central panel of *The Ghent Alterpiece*

The lamb at the center of the altarpiece is a representation of the Lamb of God, an ancient symbol for Christ (John 1:29, Revelation 5:6ff.). Christ, whose blood was shed for us, is associated with the sacrificial lamb of Passover, whose blood spared the Hebrew people from the angel of death. During the Eucharist, at the breaking of the bread, the early Christian hymn *Agnus Dei*—Lamb of God—is often sung.

God then,
encompassing all things, is
defenseless? Omnipotence
has been tossed away, reduced
to a wisp of damp wool?

And we,
frightened, bored, wanting
only to sleep till catastrophe
has raged, clashed, seethed and gone by without us,
wanting then
to awaken in quietude without remembrance of agony,

we who in shamefaced private hope
had looked to be plucked from fire and given
a bliss we deserved for having imagined it,

is it implied that we
must protect this perversely weak
animal, whose muzzle's nudgings
suppose there is milk to be found in us?
Must hold to our icy hearts
a shivering God?

So be it.
Come, rag of pungent
quiverings,
dim start.
Let's try
if something human still
can shield you,
spark
of remote light.

Denise Levertov

Lamb of God,

who takes away
the sin of the world,
have mercy on us.

From *Agnus Dei*

TRUST IN GOD

God is my light and my salvation; whom shall I fear? God is the stronghold of my life; of whom should I be afraid?

Psalm 27:1

I Am a Jew

I am a Jew and will be a Jew forever.
Even if I should die from hunger,
never will I submit.
I will always fight for my people,
on my honor.
I will never be ashamed of them,
I give my word.

I am proud of my people,
how dignified they are.
Even though I am suppressed,
I will always come back to life.

Franta Bass

*Franta Bass was one of the Jewish
children in Terezin. He died at Auschwitz
at the age of 14 in October 1944.*

Anonymous, *Sailboat*

Jewish children in the Terezin concentration camp used whatever materials were at hand to give expression to their despair and their hope.

God is my light and my salvation; whom shall I fear?

David F. Johnson, *Ellie and Raymond,* from We See Face to Face Exhibition, portraits of homeless people with AIDS, at Bailey House, New York City

GOD IS MY LIGHT AND MY SALVATION; WHOM SHALL I FEAR?

I want to write about hospitals and not being able to sleep all night and 200 pills you have to take each day in a certain order because the really nasty-tasting ones you save for the end. And how strangers blithely mention people who have died around you. And how all you want when you're in the hospital is a hot shower and someone to muscularly wash your hair, put on talcum powder and change the sweaty sheets.

God I could go on.

Oh Donna, I can't say I'm losing it, but I sure do get scared sometimes. Also, I feel like a watched pot sometimes with people around me looking at me like I'm going to explode any minute. God, the patience and strength really does have to come from within and I've certainly gotten in touch with "within" this year, but it doesn't always seem to be there. It's a mighty lesson I'm going through I feel, and you know what? There's no doubt I'm up to the challenge: I've got the strength, physically and certainly mentally. I really know that this AIDS scare is really just asking me to finally admit that I'm a lovely, wonderful human being. A source of joy—and the more I realize that, the better and calmer I'll feel. So there.

God, this makes sense, I think maybe that's what crises are for—to get us to realize and appreciate our worth.

William Dean Clark, excerpt from a January 26, 1993, letter. Bill died on February 12, 1993, in Graduate Hospital, Philadelphia.

There is dignity here—
    we will exalt it.
There is courage here—
    we will support it.

There is humanity here—
    we will enjoy it.
There is a universe in every child—
    we will share in it.
There is a voice calling through
    the chaos of our times;
there is a spirit moving across
    the waters of our world;
there is movement,
    a light,
    a promise of hope.
Let them that have ears to hear,
hear.
    But
look not for
Armageddon,
nor listen for a trumpet.
Behold, we bring you tidings of great joy:
the incarnation.

Philip Andrews

WHAT GOD REQUIRES

God has told you, O mortal, what is good; and what does God require of you but to do justice, and to love kindness, and to walk humbly with your God?

Micah 6:8

Called as Partners in Christ's Service

Called as partners in Christ's service,
Called to ministries of grace,
We respond with deep commitment
Fresh new lines of faith to trace.
May we learn the art of sharing,
Side by side and friend with friend,
Equal partners in our caring
To fulfill God's chosen end.

Christ's example, Christ's inspiring,
Christ's clear call to work and worth,
Let us follow, never faltering,
Reconciling folk on earth.
Men and women, richer, poorer,
All God's people, young and old,
Blending human skills together
Gracious gifts from God unfold.

Thus new patterns for Christ's mission,
In a small or global sense,
Help us bear each other's burdens,
Breaking down each wall or fence.
Words of comfort, words of vision,
Words of challenge, said with care,
Bring new power and strength for action,
Make us colleagues, free and fair.

So God grant us for tomorrow
Ways to order human life
That surround each person's sorrow
With a calm that conquers strife.
Make us partners in our living,
Our compassion to increase,
Messengers of faith, thus giving
Hope and confidence and peace.

Jane Parker Huber

Maerten van Heemskerck, *Tobit Burying the Dead, Feeding the Poor, and Visiting Prisoners*

Tobit was a devout Jew living in the time of Dispersion that followed the Babylonian Exile of the Jewish people. He attended faithfully to those in need as this image illustrates. His story may be found in the book of Tobit, which is in the Apocrypha.

Micah is the voice of the village peasant against the rapacious power of the state. . . . The peasants watched carefully the growing and shameless power of the Jerusalem government. That urban-scientific-military-industrial establishment had usurped the well-being of the little people.

Walter Brueggemann

Jack Kurtz, *Soup Kitchen*

Most of these students were born and raised in poor barrios and had become active pastoral agents in the process of liberation. They knew their own people and had learned to think with one eye on the gospel and one eye on the painful reality they shared with these people. They worked in their various districts and countries as catechists, social workers, or project coordinators. The way in which these young Christians spoke about their Lord was so direct and fearless that it became clear that their pastoral work among the poor was not based on any mere idea or theory but on a deep, personal experience of the presence of a loving God in the midst of the struggle for justice and peace. There was joy and gratitude; there was warm friendship and generosity; there was humility and mutual care, and these gifts were received from the Lord who had called them to be his witnesses among a suffering people.

Henri Nouwen

What good is it,
my brothers and sisters,
if you say you have
faith but do not have works?
Can faith save you?
If a brother or sister is naked
and lacks daily food,
and one of you says to them,
"Go in peace; keep warm and eat your fill,"
and yet you do not supply
their bodily needs,
what is the good of that?
So faith by itself,
if it has no works, is dead.

James 2:14–17

Epiphany 5

SHINE!

Let your LIGHT

Let your light shine before others.

Matthew 5:16b

SHINE

Give to each of us a candle of the Spirit, O God,
  as we go down into the deeps of our being.
Show us the hidden things, the creatures of our dreams,
  the storehouse of forgotten memories and hurts.
Take us down to the spring of life,
  and tell each one of us our nature and our name.
Give us freedom to grow in order that we each may become that self,
  the seed of which you planted in us at our making.
Out of the deeps we cry to you, O God.

Jim Cotter

130

Kim Woong, *The Coming of the Light*

Jesus Is the Light

Jesus is the light
of the struggle
of the oppressed
Jesus is the light
for all those
who seek justice
Jesus is the light
for all those
who love mercy
Jesus is the light
for all those
who will let
their own light shine.

Benjamin Chavis, Jr.

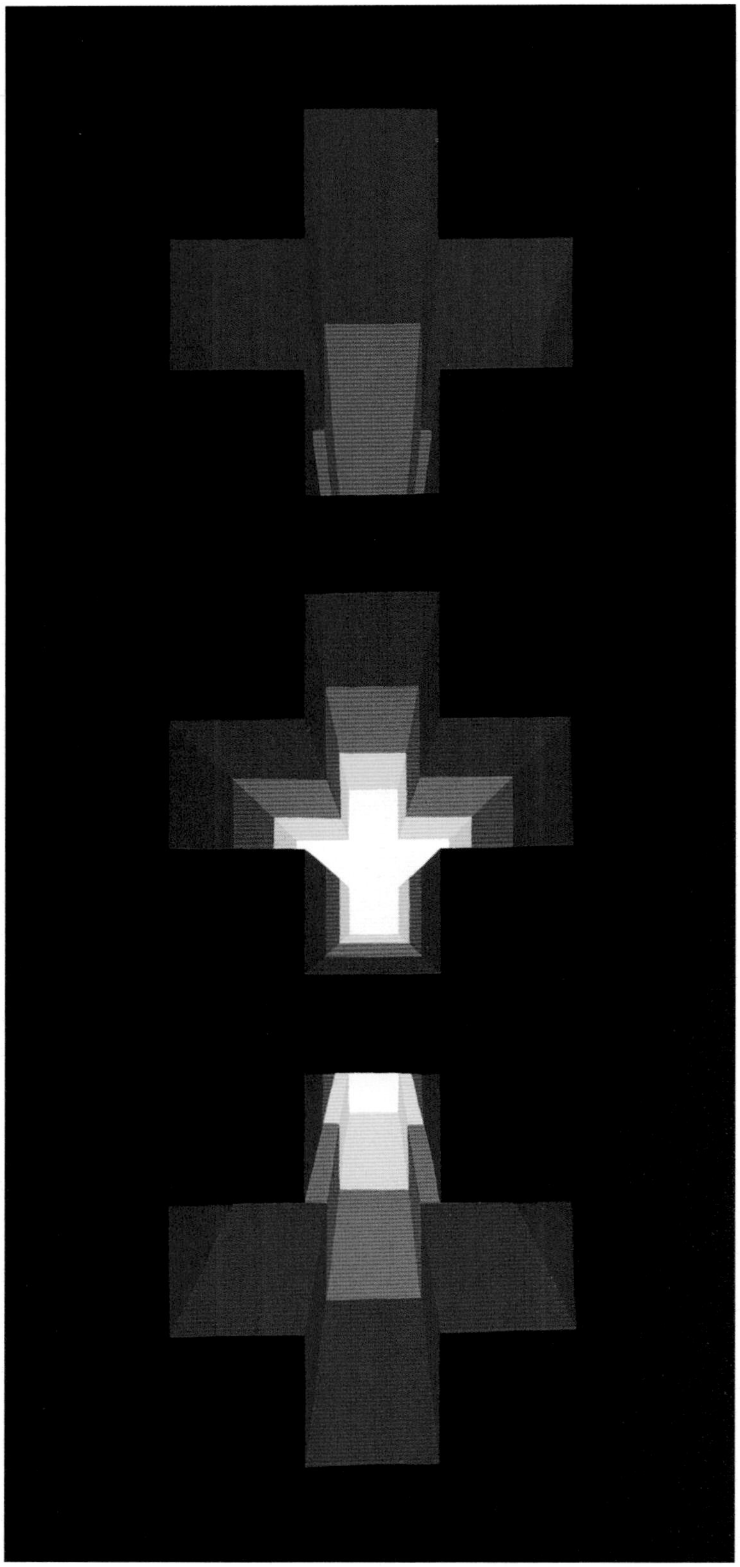

Clifford A. Ames, *Untitled*

Kim Woong,
The Coming of the Light,
detail

Matthew stresses

that the disciples' light,

which is meant

to be seen by all…

can be smothered only

by the disciples' own failure….

The disciples can cause

the failure of their mission

if they ignore others

and live only for themselves.

John P. Meier

This little light of mine,
　　I'm gonna let it shine.
Every day, every day,
　　I let my little light shine.
On Monday,
　　Gave me a gift.
On Tuesday,
　　He's come from up above.
On Wednesday,
　　Told me to have more faith.
On Thursday,
　　Gave me a little more grace.
On Friday,
　　Told me to watch and pray.
On Saturday,
　　Told me just what to say.
On Sunday,
　　Gave me a power divine.
To let my little light shine.
This little light of mine,
　　I'm gonna let it shine.
Every day, every day,
　　I let my little light shine.

African American Traditional

You gotta stay

BRIGHT to be the

LIGHT OF THE WORLD

Stephen Schwartz

GROWING IN GOD

What then is Apollos? What is Paul? Servants through whom you came to believe, as the Lord assigned to each. I planted, Apollos watered, but only God gave the growth. So neither the one who plants nor the one who waters is anything, but only God who gives the growth.

1 Corinthians 3:5–7

Be a gardener.
Dig a ditch
toil and sweat,
and turn the earth upside down
and seek the deepness
and water the plants in time.
Continue this labor
and make sweet floods to run
and noble and abundant fruits
to spring.
Take this food and drink
and carry it to God
as your true worship.

Julian of Norwich

Rex Goreleigh, *Planting* (opposite)

goreleigh. 53

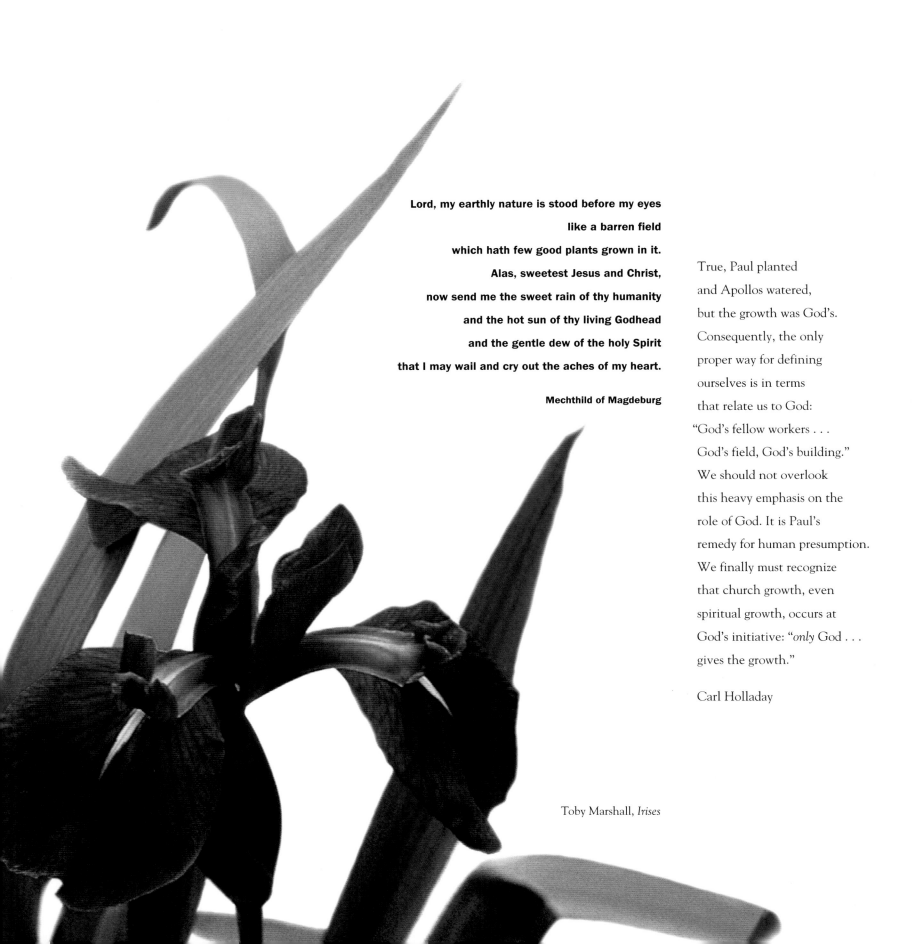

Lord, my earthly nature is stood before my eyes

like a barren field

which hath few good plants grown in it.

Alas, sweetest Jesus and Christ,

now send me the sweet rain of thy humanity

and the hot sun of thy living Godhead

and the gentle dew of the holy Spirit

that I may wail and cry out the aches of my heart.

Mechthild of Magdeburg

True, Paul planted
and Apollos watered,
but the growth was God's.
Consequently, the only
proper way for defining
ourselves is in terms
that relate us to God:
"God's fellow workers . . .
God's field, God's building."
We should not overlook
this heavy emphasis on the
role of God. It is Paul's
remedy for human presumption.
We finally must recognize
that church growth, even
spiritual growth, occurs at
God's initiative: "*only* God . . .
gives the growth."

Carl Holladay

Toby Marshall, *Irises*

The Garden Hymn

Words: Jeremiah Ingalls

Music: Johnson

The Lord in-to his gar-den come, The spi-ces yield a rich per-fume, The spi-ces yield a rich per-fume, The li-lies grow and thrive; Re-fresh-ing show-ers of grace di-vine, From Je-sus flow to ev-ery vine, From Je-sus flow to ev-ery vine, Which make the dead re-vive.

Growing in God

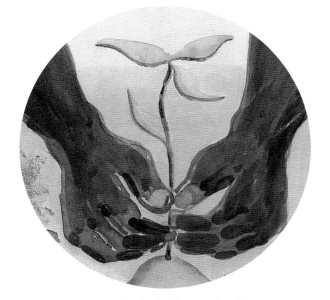

Rex Goreleigh, *Planting*, detail

WE WERE WITNESSES

For we did not follow clearly devised myths when we made known to you the power and coming of our Lord Jesus, but we have been eyewitnesses of Jesus' majesty. For Jesus received honor and glory from God when that voice was conveyed by the Majestic Glory, saying, "This is my child, my Beloved, with whom I am well pleased." We ourselves heard this voice come from heaven, while we were with Jesus on the holy mountain.

2 Peter 1:16–18

"I have never seen him like this," Peter said to John.

Transfiguration (Vie de Jesus Mafa)

When they reached the mountaintop, Jesus with his arms extended was dancing and laughing and calling out to Elijah to carry him home. The wind was blowing and the dust he kicked up swirled around him like a great cloud. The sun blazed behind him so that they had to squint to see him.

"I have never seen him like this," Peter said to John.

"Nor I. Isn't it wonderful?" John and James took Jesus by the hand and they circled and danced together.

"Master," Peter called to Jesus, "let us never leave this place. Let's stay here forever. Let us set up our tents . . . in Galilee."

They sat down to rest. The effort had exhausted all of them. They were still breathing heavily yet still relishing the magnificent moment.

"Master," Peter said again. "Why not stay here?" He tried not to look in the direction Jesus had set his gaze, south toward Jerusalem.

The sun was setting. It had been an extraordinary and eventful day. They were tired and happy. Jesus stared toward Jerusalem.

"There is one more mountain to climb," he said. "In Jerusalem."

John Aurelio

David C. Driskell,
Movement, The Mountain

The colors, forms,
and their arrangement
suggest the possibility of
transformation going on
before one's eyes.

The sun's golden

splendour

now sunders

the night,

And shatters

the power

of the evil one's

might.

Wolfgang Amadeus Mozart

"You got a secret need," the blind man said. "Them that know Jesus once can't escape Him in the end."

"I ain't never known Him," Haze said.

"You got at least knowledge," the blind man said. "That's enough. You know His name and you're marked. If Jesus has marked you there ain't nothing you can do about it. Them that have knowledge can't swap it for ignorance."

Flannery O'Connor

[God], transfigure our perception

With the purest light that shines,

And recast our life's intentions

To the shape of Your designs,

Till we seek no other glory

Than what lies past Calvary's hill

And our living and our dying

And our rising

by Your will.

Thomas H. Troeger

Lent

José Faustino Altramirano,
Blessed Is He, detail

We study the world in its reality—

its temptations,

its shadows, its betrayals.

The season of Lent begins on Ash Wednesday. Vestiges of the early church's experience of public penance still exist in the ceremony of ashes placed on the foreheads of the penitents with the remonstrance: "Remember you are dust and unto dust you shall return." The weeks that followed were a time of intense reflection, self-scrutiny, and preparation for reincorporation into the community from which one was estranged by sin. For us, where public penance is not so common, Lent may provide a time for community and individual preparation for following Jesus on the most difficult of paths, the path of self-sacrificing love.

Vestiges of other ancient traditions are present in Lent as well. The Gospels were used to give the final instructions to the catechumens as they prepared to be baptized into the church at the Easter Vigil on the Saturday night before Easter morning. The stories from John of the man born blind, the Samaritan woman, and the raising of Lazarus challenge us to engage essential questions of faith in Jesus—in who he is, and how one comes to faith in him.

All of Lent leads to Holy Week, the week in which Jesus enters Jerusalem and faces death. It begins on Palm Sunday with the triumphal entrance of Jesus into the city, acclaimed as its ruler. The stories of Holy Week proceed through the poignance of the Last Supper with his friends in which he charges them with the ministry of service and is betrayed by one of his own. Finally, witnessing his death on the cross, the followers of Jesus are confronted with the stark reality of the cost of discipleship. Embracing our humanity, Jesus embraced both our life and our death.

Purple is the color of Lent, but Holy Week is framed in the red and black of the Passion of Palm Sunday and Good Friday.

Today Lent is a time of intensive preparation for us all. We study the world in its reality—its temptations, its shadows, its betrayals. We fast and pray and engage in spiritual preparation to follow Jesus faithfully to the end. We open ourselves to Jesus' love; we try to live up to it.

JESUS EMBRACED OUR LIFE AND DEATH

CREATE IN ME A CLEAN HEART

Create in me a clean heart, O God, and put a new and right spirit within me. Cast me not away from thy presence, and take not thy holy Spirit from me. Restore to me the joy of thy salvation, and uphold me with a willing spirit.

Psalm 51:10–12

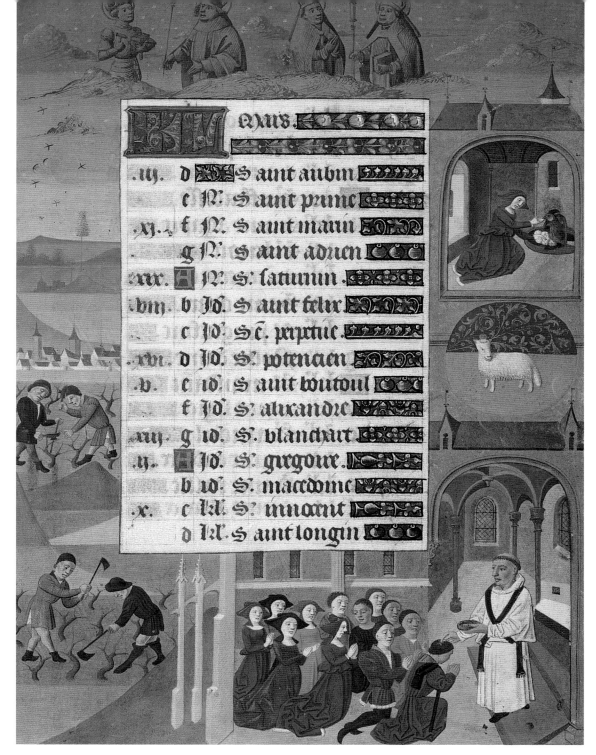

Illuminated manuscript, *Receiving Ashes*

Ash Wednesday. There is no other day like Ash Wednesday. The proud and the meek, the arrogant and the humble are all made equal on Ash Wednesday. The healthy and the sick, the assured and the sick in spirit, all make their way to church in the gray morning or in the dusty afternoon. They line up silently, eyes downcast, bony fingers counting the beads of the rosary, lips mumbling prayers. All are repentant, all are preparing themselves for the shock of the laying of the ashes on the forehead and the priest's agonizing words, "Thou art dust, and to dust thou shalt return."

Rudolfo A. Anaya

Sanders Nicolson, *Untitled*

Skin was earth; it was soil. I could see, even on my own skin, the joined trapezoids of dust specks God had wetted and stuck with his spit the morning he made Adam from dirt. Now, all these generations later, we people could still see on our skin the inherited prints of the dust specks of Eden.

I loved this thought, and repeated it for myself often. I don't know where I got it; my parents cited Adam and Eve only in jokes. Someday I would count the trapezoids, with the aid of a mirror, and learn precisely how many dust specks Adam comprised—one single handful God wetted, shaped, blew into, and set firmly into motion and left to wander about in the fabulous garden bewildered.

Annie Dillard

The following or similar words may be spoken:

Friends in Christ,
every year at the time of the Christian Passover
we celebrate our redemption
through the death and resurrection
of our Lord Jesus Christ.
Lent is a time to prepare for this celebration
and to renew our life in the paschal mystery.
We begin this holy season
by remembering our need for repentance,
and for the mercy and forgiveness
proclaimed in the gospel of Jesus Christ.

If ashes are used the following may be said:

We begin our journey to Easter with the sign of ashes,
an ancient sign,
that speaks of the frailty and uncertainty of human life,
and marks the penitence of this community.

The minister continues:

I invite you therefore, in the name of the Lord,
to observe a holy Lent
by self-examination, penitence, prayer,
fasting, and almsgiving,
and by reading and meditating on the word of God.
Let us bow before our creator and redeemer.

A brief silence is observed.

Anglican Church of Canada, *The Book of Alternative Services*

Imposition of Ashes

Let us pray.

Almighty God,
you have created us out of the dust of the earth;
may these ashes be to us
a sign of our mortality and penitence,
so we may remember that only by your gracious gift
are we given everlasting life;
through Jesus Christ our Savior. Amen.

Anglican Church of Canada, *The Book of Alternative Services*

We Are Dust

We are dust in pain.
The light shines through us
as through-wave spray, dust of water
breaking, or the falling rain.

Ursula K. LeGuin

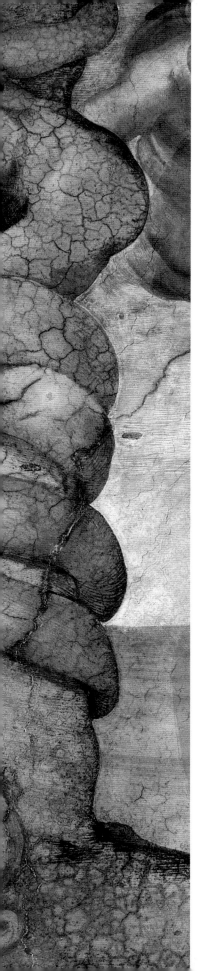

T E M P T E D

God said, "You shall not eat of the fruit of the tree that is in the middle of the garden, nor shall you touch it, or you shall die." But the serpent said to the woman, "You will not die; for God knows that when you eat of it your eyes will be opened, and you will be like God, knowing good and evil."

Genesis 3:3–5

All the old primitive sins are not dead, but are crouching in the… corners of our modern hearts.

Carl Gustav Jung

Michelangelo Buonarotti,
Original Sin and Expulsion from Paradise (Fall of Man)

Let us Pray.

I saw the pale student of unhallowed arts kneeling beside the thing he had put together. . . . Frightful must it be, for supremely frightful would be the effect of any human endeavor to mock the stupendous mechanism of the Creator of the world.

Mary Shelley, *Frankenstein*

Boris Karloff as the Frankenstein Monster

Because the world is beautiful,
and beauty is a tender thing,
and we are stewards of creation,
we need you, God.
We need you, God.

Because Human knowledge seems endless,
and we do not know what we do not know,
we need you, God.
We need you, God.

Because we cannot live without you
and are free to go against you,
and could worship our wisdom alone,
we need you, God.
We need you, God.

Because you came among us,
and sat beside us,
and healed our pain and let us wound you,
and loved us to the end,
and triumphed over all our hatred,
we need you, God.
We need you, God.
Amen

Iona Community Worship Book

"What's best and worst?" Atkin asked, casually.
"Best makes us long-term happy,
worst makes us long-term sorry."
"How long-term?"
"Years. A lifetime."

Richard Bach

Carl Mansfield, *No Swimming Allowed*

But I want to!
Standing-nervous
-jump-jump?
The fateful choice
 is about to be made.

Si fui motivo de dolor, oh Dios;
si por mi causa el débil tropezó;
si en tus caminos yo no quise andar,
¡perdón, oh Dios!

If I have been the source of pain, O God;
If to the weak I have refused my strength;
If, in rebellion, I have strayed away;
Forgive me, God.

Sara M. de Hall,
based on a text by C. M. Battersby,
translated by Janet W. May

BORN FROM ABOVE

Now there was a Pharisee named Nicodemus, a leader of the Jews. He came to Jesus by night and said, "Rabbi, we know that you are a teacher who has come from God; for no one can do these signs that you do apart from the presence of God." Jesus answered him, "Very truly, I tell you, no one can see the dominion of God without being born from above."

John 3:1–3

Dear God,

I know all about where babies come from. I think. From inside mommies and daddies put them there. Where are they before that? Do you have them in heaven? How do they get here? Do you have to take care of them all first? Please answer all my questions. I always think of you.

Yours truly,

Susan

From *Children's Letters to God: The New Collection*

"Who are you?"

she exclaimed, as the vision brightened into a form distinct, beaming with the beauty of holiness, and radiant with love. She then said, audibly addressing the mysterious visitant—"I *know* you, and I *don't* know you."

Meaning, "You seem perfectly familiar; I feel that you not only love me, but that you always *have* loved me—yet I know you not—I cannot call you by name." When she said, "I know you," the subject of the vision remained distinct and quiet. When she said, "I don't know you," it moved restlessly about, like agitated waters. So while she repeated, without intermission, "I know you, I know you," that the vision might remain— "Who are you?" was the cry of her heart, and her whole soul was in one deep prayer that this heavenly personage might be revealed to her, and remain with her. At length, after bending both soul and body with the intensity of this desire, till breath and strength seemed failing, and she could maintain her position no longer, an answer came to her, saying distinctly, "It is Jesus." "Yes," she responded, "it is *Jesus*."

Sojourner Truth

Eero Saarinen and Associates, architects,
*Kresge Chapel, Massachusetts Institute
of Technology*

Light on a brass screen designed
by Harry Bertoia moves the gaze
from chapel alter to the sky above.

John LaFarge, *Visit of Nicodemus to Christ*

"You are only afraid because you don't know anything about death.... But someday you will wonder why you were afraid, even as today you wonder why you feared to be born."

"What is death?" Kino asked.

"Death is the great gateway," Kino's father said. His face was not at all sad. Instead, it was quiet and happy.

"The gateway—where?" Kino asked again.

Kino's father smiled. "Can you remember when you were born?"

Kino shook his head. "I was too small."

Kino's father laughed. "I remember very well. Oh, how hard you thought it was to be born! You cried and you screamed."

"Didn't I want to be born?" Kino asked. This was very interesting to him.

"You did not know anything about it and so you were afraid of it," his father replied. "But see how foolish you were! Here we were waiting for you, your parents, already loving you and eager to welcome you. And you have been very happy, haven't you?"

"Until the big wave came," Kino replied. "Now I am afraid again because of the death that the big wave brought."

"You are only afraid because you don't know anything about death," his father replied. "But someday you will wonder why you were afraid, even as today you wonder why you feared to be born."

Pearl S. Buck

My God, I need to have signs of your grace.
Give me your sacraments,
the first fruits of your Kingdom.

I thirst for smiles
    for sweet odors,
    for soft words,
    for firm gestures,
    for truth and goodness,
    and for triumphs
    (no matter how small)
    of justice.

You know, O God, how hard it is to survive captivity
without any hope of the Holy City.
Sing to us, God, the songs of the promised land.
Serve us your manna in the desert.

Let there be, in some place,
a community of men, women, elderly, children, and new-
    born babies
    as a first fruit,
    as our appetizer,
    and our embrace of the future.

Amen.

Rubem A. Alves

A Samaritan woman came to draw water, and Jesus said to her, "Give me a drink." (The disciples had gone to the city to buy food.) The Samaritan woman said to Jesus, "How is it that you, a Jew, ask a drink of me, a woman of Samaria?" (Jews do not share things in common with Samaritans.) Jesus answered her, "If you knew the gift of God, and who it is that is saying to you, 'Give me a drink,' you would have asked that one, who would then have given you living water."

John 4:7–10

Jesus and the Samaritan Woman, Catacomb of Via Latina

[The] Use of the symbol of water shows how realistically John thought of eternal life: water is to natural life as living water is to eternal life.

Raymond Brown

A Psalm of Living Water

Leader: *You are like a mountain spring,*
O Fountain of Living Water.

All: **I sip from the deep down freshness of Your never-failing love.**

Leader: *You are like a summer rain,*
O Sudden Benediction,

All: **drench my soul and quench my thirsting spirit with Your peace.**

Leader: *You are like a raging sea,*
O Storm Upon my Ocean,

All: **breaking into bits my fragile bark as I learn to lean on You.**

Leader: *You are like a waterfall,*
Oasis in my Desert:

All: **source of my heart's survival in the press and stress of life.**

Leader: *You are like a cleansing flood,*
River of Reconciliation:

All: **washing away the selfish self-serving signs of my sinfulness.**

Leader: *You are like a bottomless well,*
O Cup of Lifegiving Water:

All: **full up to overflowing. Praise be to You, Shaddai.**

Miriam Therese Winter

Manuel Alvarez Bravo, *The Public Fountain*

In the name of God,
In the name of Jesus,
In the name of Spirit,
The perfect Three of power.

The little drop of the Father
On thy little forehead, beloved one.

The little drop of the Son
On thy little forehead, beloved one.

The little drop of the Spirit
On thy little forehead, beloved one.

To aid thee, to guard thee,
To shield thee, to surround thee.

...

The little drop of the Three
To fill thee with Their pleasantness.

The little drop of the Three
To fill thee with Their virtue.

O the little drop of the Three
To fill thee with Their virtue.

Esther de Waal

A custom of early Celtic Christianity
was a form of baptismal blessing
of a child immediately after its birth
by the mother and the midwives
who attended her. This preceded the
formal baptism in the church,
which took place eight days later.

Let God's love flow through me.

My Lord is the source of Love; I the river's course.
Let God's love flow through me. I will not obstruct it.
Irrigation ditches can water but a portion of the field;
the great Yangtze River can water a thousand acres.
Expand my heart, O Lord, that I may love yet more people.
The waters of love can water vast tracts,
nothing will be lost to me.
The greater the outward flow, the greater the returning tide.
If I am not linked to Love's source, I will dry up.
If I dam the waters of Love, they will stagnate.
Can I compare my heart to the boundless seas?
But abandon not the measure of my heart, O Lord.
Let the waves of your love still billow there!

Wang Weifan

7hen the Pharisees also began to ask the man who had

been blind how he had received his sight. He said to them, "Jesus put mud

on my eyes. Then I washed, and now I see." Some of the Pharisees said,

"This man is not from God, for he does not observe the sabbath." But others

said, "How can a man who is a sinner perform such signs?" And they were

divided. So they said again to the man who had been blind, "What do

you say about Jesus? It was your eyes he opened."

John 9:15–17b

According to the Gospels, Jesus' miracles were real, specific, and discernible events. Yet they occurred in an atmosphere of eschatological expectation and faith. When wrenched from this context, they look like the works of a magician or sorcerer. In his own time and in the earliest church the question of miracle could not be separated from faith in Jesus' preaching and power, both of which had to do with the kingdom of God. Faith could not, and cannot prove the miracles happened; faith provides the context in which their meaning can be discussed.

Robert A. Spivey and D. Moody Smith

Elijah Pierce, *The Man That Was Born Blind Restored to Sight*

Mark Rothko, Rothko Chapel, Houston, Texas

The huge paintings created for the Rothko Chapel appear to be unrelieved shadows, yet as the viewer meditates upon them, central textured images of the cross may reveal themselves.

It was your eyes he opened.

We walked down the path to the well-house, attracted by the fragrance of the honeysuckle with which it was covered. Someone was drawing water and my teacher placed my hand under the spout. As the cool stream gushed over one hand she spelled into the other the word water, first slowly, then rapidly. I stood still, my whole attention fixed upon the motions of her fingers. Suddenly I felt a misty consciousness as of something forgotten—a thrill of returning thought; and somehow the mystery of language was revealed to me. I knew then that "w-a-t-e-r" meant the wonderful cool something that was flowing over my hand. That living word awakened my soul, gave it light, hope, joy, set it free! There were barriers still, it is true, but barriers that could in time be swept away.

I left the well-house eager to learn. Everything had a name, and each name gave birth to a new thought. As we returned to the house every object which I touched seemed to quiver with life. That was because I saw everything with the strange, new sight that had come to me. . . . I learned a great many new words that day. I do not remember what they all were; but I do know that *mother, father, sister, teacher* were among them—words that were to make the world blossom for me, "like Aaron's rod, with flowers." It would have been difficult to find a happier child than I was as I lay in my crib at the close of that eventful day and lived over the joys it had brought me, and for the first time longed for a new day to come.

Helen Keller

Lord, since long, long ago, innumerable times I have thought of your face. Especially since coming to this country have I done so tens of times. When I was in hiding in the mountains of Tomogi; when I crossed over in the little ship, when I wandered in the mountains; when I lay in prison at night. . . . Whenever I prayed your face appeared before me; when I was alone I thought of your face imparting a blessing; when I was captured your face as it appeared when you carried your cross gave me life. This face is deeply ingrained in my soul—the most beautiful, the most precious thing in the world has been living in my heart.

Shusaku Endo

he hand of God came upon me, and God brought

me out by the spirit of God and set me down in the

middle of a valley; it was full of bones. God led me

all around them; there were very many lying in the

valley, and they were very dry. God said to me,

"Mortal, can these bones live? I will lay sinews on

you, and will cause flesh to come upon you, and

cover you with skin, and put breath in you, and you

shall live, and you shall know that I am God."

Ezekiel 37:1–3b, 6

Frank Day, *Mourning at Mineral Springs*

Exile is death. It is a valley where all the prophet can see are bones, where he alone has eyes to see and hear the question too horrible to be answered except by God, "Can these bones live?" "[God], you know." The place of exile is not just the north country, or a new Egypt, or the regions around the earth's boundaries, north, south, east, and west. It is as cold and final as the tomb, where no breath is drawn. . . . Yes, Israel is totally dead. . . . The valley is full of bones, and all are very dry. Not one shows any sign of stirring by its own effort. The prophet sees a wasteland, still, lifeless, and all encompassing. His words of judgment have reached as far as they can, until he alone is left—or, better, he alone with God whose hand first sent him on this grim mission.

Christopher R. Seitz

ncalled, unrobed, unanointed . . . Baby Suggs, holy, followed by every black man, woman and child who could make it through, took her great heart to the Clearing. . . .

After situating herself on a huge flat-sided rock, Baby Suggs bowed her head and prayed silently. The company watched her from the trees. They knew she was ready when she put her stick down. Then she shouted, "Let the children come!" and they ran from the trees toward her.

"Let your mothers hear you laugh," she told them, and the woods rang. The adults looked on and could not help smiling.

Then "Let the grown men come," she shouted. They stepped out one by one from among the ringing trees.

"Let your wives and your children see you dance," she told them, and ground life shuddered under their feet.

Finally she called the women to her. "Cry," she told them. "For the living and the dead. Just cry." And without covering their eyes the women let loose.

It started that way: laughing children, dancing men, crying women and then it got mixed up. Women stopped crying and danced; men sat down and cried; children danced, women laughed, children cried until, exhausted and riven, all and each lay about the Clearing damp and gasping for breath. In the silence that followed, Baby Sugg, holy, offered up to them her great big heart.

She did not tell them to clean up their lives or to go and sin no more. She did not tell them they were the blessed of the earth, its inheriting meek or its glorybound pure.

She told them that the only grace they could have was the grace they could imagine. That if they could not see it, they would not have it.

"Here," she said, "in this here place, we flesh; flesh that weeps, laughs; flesh that dances on bare feet in grass. Love it. Love it hard. Yonder they do not love your flesh. They despise it. . . . It is flesh I'm talking about here. Flesh that needs to be loved. Feet that need to rest and dance; backs that need support; shoulders that need arms, strong arms I'm telling you. And O my people, out yonder, hear me, they do not love your neck unnoosed and straight. So love your neck; put a hand on it, stroke it and hold it up. . . . The beat and beating heart, love that too. . . . Love your heart. . . .

Saying no more, she stood up then and danced with her twisted hip the rest of what her heart had to say while the others opened their mouths and gave her the music. Long notes held until the four-part harmony was perfect enough for their deeply loved flesh.

Toni Morrison

Beseeching the breath of the divine one,
His life-giving breath,
His breath of old age,
His breath of waters,
His breath of seeds,
His breath of riches,
His breath of fecundity,
His breath of power,
His breath of good fortune,
Asking for his breath
And into my warm body drawing his breath,
I add to your breath
That happily you may always live.

Zuni Chant

David Hiser, *Day of the Dead Celebrations*

The Day of the Dead in Mexico mocks the clear boundaries between life and death and celebrates the still lively and engaged presence of those who have lived before us.

Prayer from *Litany of the Four Elements*

Leader: God of earth, air, fire, and water,
we surrender to you our old humanity.

All: Christ, we would rise with you:
we would be born anew.

Leader: Christ has died: Christ is risen.
We are forgiven: we too may leave the grave.

Kate Compston

Paul Vozdic, *Dancer in Motion* (opposite)

BLESSED IS THE ONE

When they had come near Jerusalem and had reached Bethphage at the Mount of Olives, Jesus sent two disciples, saying to them, "Go into the village ahead of you, and immediately you will find a donkey tied, and a colt with her; untie them and bring them to me." The crowds that went ahead of him and that followed were shouting, "Hosanna to the Son of David! Blessed is the one who comes in the name of God! Hosanna in the highest heaven!"

Matthew 21:1–2, 9

Hosanna

Mantos y palmas esparciendo va el pueblo alegre de Jerusalén.
Allá a lo lejos se empieza a mirar en un pollino al hijo de Dios.

Mientras mil voces resuenan por doquier; Hosanna al que viene en el nombre del Señor.
Con un aliento de gran exclamación prorrumpen con voz triunfal:
"¡Hosanna, ¡Hosanna al Rey! ¡Hosanna, ¡Hosanna al Rey!"

Mantles and branches from the tall palm trees
cover the streets of Jerusalem.
There in the distance we begin to see
on a humble donkey, the son of God.

Rubén Ruiz, translated by Gertrude C. Suppe

Giotto, *Entry into Jerusalem*

This is one of a cycle of stories about Jesus told on the walls of the Arena Chapel in Padua, Italy, through the use of frescoes.

Who is this riding among us?
Jesus, the Prophet of Nazareth.

Blessed is he who comes in the name of God.
Hosanna, may his Way be victorious.

Who is this riding the animal of peace?
Jesus, the Prophet of Nazareth.

Blessed be the freedom he brings.
Hosanna, may his Way be victorious.

Who is this carrying the palm of peace?
Jesus, the Prophet of Nazareth.

Blessed be our leader, the Prince of peace.
Hosanna, may his Way be victorious.

Who is this that destroys the weapons of war?
Jesus, the Prophet of Nazareth.

Blessed is he who comes in the name of God.
Hosanna, may his Way be victorious.

Who is this that frees the oppressed from prison?
Jesus, the Prophet of Nazareth.

Blessed is he who releases all captives.
Hosanna, may his Way be victorious.

Who is this that makes wars to cease in all the world?
Jesus, the Prophet of Nazareth.

Blessed is he who restores the Paradise of Eden.
Hosanna, may his Way be victorious.

"The Covenant of Peace — A Liberation Prayer"

Blessed is the one who comes in the name of God!

Little grey donkey, Little grey donkey, Little grey donkey, Ho.

Do you know just who it is you carry on your back?

'Tis no ordinary load, no mean or common pack.

You are blessed of all beasts to carry into town

Christ the Lord of Galilee; He wears no earthly crown.

Little grey donkey, Little grey donkey, Little grey donkey, Ho.

Once you were a simple beast of poor and lowly state.

Christ Himself hath chosen you and honoured is your fate.

Though your path with palms is spread, make haste along the way;

You were destined here to ride on this triumphal day.

Little grey donkey, Little grey donkey, Little grey donkey, Ho.

Yonder is a grassy hill; it's known as Calvary.

Up against the cloudless sky a barren cross you see.

Little grey donkey, Little grey mare, don't hide your head in shame.

For you bear the Lamb of God, and Jesus is His name.

For you bear the Lamb of God, and Jesus is His name.

Natalie Sleeth

José Faustino Altramirano, *Blessed Is He*

At first it appeared that his return to Jerusalem was a triumph rather than the beginning of the events that would lead to his death. People cut branches from the trees and strewed them in front of him. Others spread their cloaks on the road. And he was surrounded by cries of "Hosannah to the son of David! Blessed is he who comes in the name of the Lord. Hosannah in the Highest."

How easily and how terribly "Hosannah!" changed to "Crucify him! Crucify him!"

Madeleine L'Engle

THE LAST SUPPER

While they were eating, Jesus took a loaf of bread, and after blessing it he broke it, gave it to the disciples, and said, "Take, eat; this is my body." Then he took a cup, and after giving thanks he gave it to them, saying, "Drink from it, all of you; for this is my blood of the covenant, which is poured out for many for the forgiveness of sins."

Matthew 26:26–28

Annette Gandy Fortt, *The Last Supper*

Friends meeting
one final time
in life as he knew it.
The thought of things
presently to come
weighing heavily
on his heart.
And others seeing
no more nor less
than what wine-dulled sense
can glean from appearances:
something they had done
with predicted regularity
long before this
momentous time arrived.
Gathered with friends,
celebrating that
passing-over event.
My how time flies
a good time!
Minutes ticking past.
Too fast!
Too little time left!
Three years walking,
talking, teaching,
reaching out in hope
and calling forth
the good in each:
healing for
the seasoned cynic
in us all.
So now it
comes down to this:
leave-taking.
What to say?
What to do?
So much to say,
So much to do.
All poured into this
last parting gesture:
a sign,
a prayer.
Relying on
memory's gift
and what a transformed meal
can possibly recall
celebrated
miles and years
from here and now
with people gathered
in his name.

Michael Moynahan

Jesu, Jesu

Jesu, Jesu, fill us with your love,
show us how to serve
the neighbors we have from you.

Kneels at the feet of his friends,
Silently washes their feet,
Master who pours out himself for them.

Neighbors are rich and poor,
Neighbors are black and white,
Neighbors are near and far away.

These are the ones we should serve,
These are the ones we should love,
All are neighbors to us and you.

Kneel at the feet of our friends,
Silently washing their feet,
This is the way we should live with you.

Ghana Folk Song, adapted by Tom Colvin

Carmen Lomas Garza, *Tamalada (Making Tamales)*

The image of the Last Supper finds a reflection in
the activity of the family preparing tamales.

175

AT THE CROSS

So they took Jesus;

and carrying the cross

by himself, he went

out to what is called

The Place of the Skull,

which in Hebrew

is called Golgotha.

There they crucified him.

John 19:16b–18a

Lord our God,
who by these words
from the cross
dost speak unto our souls;
let it come to us now
with assurance
and in the might of thy Spirit,
that we may see in Christ
crucified thy power and wisdom,
and the revelation
of thine infinite love.

A Book of Worship for Free Churches

Graham Sutherland, *The Crucifixion*

With one glance at the Cross
you know that Jesus experienced
the bitterest of all human pain,
that torture called rejection.
It's impossible to be gay and not
know what Jesus knew, what God
knew when men did what they
did to his son. Let me shout
it from the rooftops, Christians,
don't you ever dare speak of Christ
unless you suffer with him on his
Cross! Get that folks? It's the
Cross that makes Jesus the Christ.
Not the other way around!

Anderson Clark, letter to his son,
who died of AIDS

It's the Cross that makes Jesus the Christ.

Anderson Clark

Letting go of the symbol of the cross may make some sense on a rational level. But on a holistic level its value as a symbol is immense. Its power is its ability to embrace and thereby allow us into the full reality of suffering. Suffering cannot be confined to rationality. The experience of suffering makes no rational sense. The power of the cross as a symbol is that it helps us locate our common predicament in the world—that we experience suffering—in a common experience of God. God is so incarnate with us that God even experiences that which we experience in all its reality. God stands in solidarity with us, born out of love for us.

Kathleen T. Talvacchia

A tradition in many Protestant churches is for the sermon on Good Friday to be based on the "Seven Last Words" of Jesus from the cross —phrases and texts taken from all four passion narratives.

My God, my God

It is finished.

Woman, behold your son! Behold your mother.

Donatello, *Lamentation Over the Dead Christ*

why have you forsaken me?

thirst.

Today you shall be with me in paradise.

The cross we bear
precedes the crown we wear.
To be a Christian one must take up his cross,
with all its difficulties and agonizing
and tension-packed content
and carry it until that very cross
leaves its marks upon us and redeems us
to that more excellent way which comes
only through suffering.

Martin Luther King, Jr.

Into your hands I commend my spirit.

Forgive them; for they know not what they do.

Easter

John Biggers, *The Upper Room*

We learn again to recognize the risen Jesus

where he is to be found—in our midst,

in our stories, in the breaking of the bread.

Easter Sunday begins the fifty days of the Easter season with the story of the empty tomb and the charge by the messenger to "go and tell!" For the next forty days—until Ascension Day—Christians tell and retell stories of Jesus' first followers who encountered him against all hope—amidst doubt, fear, and longing—risen from the dead.

The efforts of the first Christian communities to spread the Gospel are recounted from the Acts of the Apostles. From Ascension Day, after Jesus leaves in triumph, his followers begin a period of prayer while awaiting the promised coming of his Spirit at Pentecost, which occurs ten days later.

The early church called these weeks after Easter *Mystagogia*. Instruction for newly baptized Christians would continue as they explored, with their new community, the joyful mystery of the encounter of the risen Christ with their lives.

The church wears celebratory white and gold during Eastertide, as we learn again to recognize the risen Jesus where he is to be found. Jesus will be found in our midst, in our stories, in the breaking of the bread—and as we faithfully bear word of the reality of Christ's presence to our world.

GO AND TELL

The angel said, "Do not be afraid;
I know that you are looking for Jesus
who was crucified. Jesus is not here;
but has raised, as Jesus said. Come, see
the place where Jesus lay. Then go
quickly and tell the disciples, 'Jesus has
been raised from the dead, and indeed
is going ahead of you to Galilee;
there you will see Jesus.' This is my
message for you."

Matthew 28:5b–7

In a setting that often made women subordinate to men, it is striking that women were the first to tell the story of Jesus' resurrection. In Matthew's story Jesus commissioned them to "go and tell" (v. 10). The risen Jesus met these joyous women on their way and greeted them. They took hold of him and worshiped him, the one in whom God was so powerfully at work and who had entrusted them with such a message.

Paul Hammer

John Biggers, *The Upper Room*

Biggers situated the "empty tomb" in the rural South of the United States and depicts its witnesses as the African American women who dwell there. His title suggests that their witness to the power of the risen Christ in their lives continues in the tradition of the weekly prayer gathering known as the "Upper Room."

Go and Tell!

The young poet of the Harlem Renaissance equates the lynching of a black man with the crucifixion.

*The young poet
of the Harlem Renaissance
equates the lynching
of a black man with
the crucifixion.*

Now God be praised that a door should creak,

And that a rusty hinge should shriek.

Of all sweet sounds that I may hear

Of lute or lyre or dulcimer,

None ever shall assail my ear

Sweet as the sound of a grating door

I had thought closed forevermore.

Out of my deep-plowed agony,

I turned to see a door swing free;

The very door he once came through

To death, now framed for us anew

His vital self, his and no other's

Live body of the dead, my brother's.

Like one who dreams within a dream,

Hand at my throat, lest I should scream,

I moved with hopeful, doubting pace

To meet the dead man face to face.

Countee Cullen

Elizabeth Catlett, *Man*

[Michelangelo] was commissioned by Metello Vari to execute "a life-sized marble figure of Christ, naked, standing, holding a cross in His arms, in whatever pose the artist judged to be suitable." Michelangelo added the other instruments of the passion, such as the sponge, the lance, the cord. Christ's wounds are minimized and he does not display them; this is the naked figure of an Apollo of noble proportions and a beautifully modeled torso. The Christ figure holds the instruments of the passion against his right side, away from the spectator and looks to his left, the side from which evil traditionally comes. This beautiful Apollonic Christ [is] both transcendent and entirely corporeal.

Jane Dillenberger

EASTER SEQUENCE

"Tell us, Mary, what you saw on the way?"

"I saw the tomb of the living Christ

and the glory of his rising;

angelic witnesses, the towel and the linen cloths.

Christ my hope is arisen;

he goes before his own to Galilee."

From Easter Sunday Mass

Michelangelo Buonarotti, *Risen Christ*

ROOM FOR DOUBT

Jesus said to Thomas, "Have you believed because you have seen me? Blessed are those who have not seen and yet have come to believe."

John 20:29

These Things Did Thomas Count as Real

These things did Thomas count as real:
The warmth of blood, the chill of steel,
The grain of wood, the heft of stone,
The last frail twitch of flesh and bone.

The vision of his skeptic mind
Was keen enough to make him blind
To any unexpected act
Too large for his small world of fact.

His reasoned certainties denied
That one could live when one had died,
Until his fingers read like Braille
The markings of the spear and nail.

...

Thomas H. Troeger

Doubt is pain
too lonely to know
that faith is his
twin brother.

Kahlil Gibran

Rembrandt Harmensz van Rijn, *Doubting Thomas*

What we are confronted with, then, is a foreign land, a passage through a desert; testing and discernment. But in this same land, from which God is not in fact absent, the seeds of a new spirituality can germinate. This spirituality gives rise to new songs to the Lord.

Gustavo Gutiérrez

May we, O God, by grace believe
and thus the risen Christ receive,
Whose raw imprinted palms reach out
And beckoned Thomas from his doubt.

Thomas H. Troeger

The Younger Brother of Thomas

Thomas really didn't touch him.
I would have.
What can you prove just by looking?
Since when is seeing believing?
They killed my brother's friend
That's fact.
And Thomas just went crazy.
I was there.
It hurt to hear him cry like that.
I don't want to go crazy like Thomas has.
And then this story starts:
that Jesus isn't dead,
that he's been seen
walking through walls,
showing up at supper time.
But nobody, nobody had touched him.
Thomas didn't buy it.
I wouldn't have either.
Never listen to an eyewitness.
Get the facts firsthand.
Don't settle for someone
you can't get a hold of.
But then this ghost or hoax appeared
and called his name.
Thomas took one look
and thought that he'd seen God.
He really didn't touch him, see.
But doubting Thomas believes.
It would take more than that
to convince me.
Doubting runs in the family.

Heather Murray Elkins

Lonnie Duka

Serious doubt is confirmation of **FAITH**

Paul Tillich

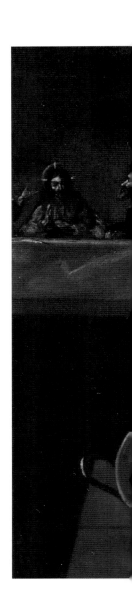

Plenty

**Having shared our bread,
we know that we are
no longer hungry. It is enough**

**that you see me for myself.
That I see you for yourself.
That we bless what we see**

**and do not borrow, do not use
one another. This is how we know
we are no longer hungry . . . that**

**the world is full of terror, full of beauty
and yet we are not afraid to find solace here.
To be bread for each other. To love.**

Gunilla Norris

Then they told me

what had happened

on the road, and

how he had been

made known to

them in the breaking

of the bread.

Luke 24:35

*Jesus Christ,
the Bread of Life,
we gather at your table
to know you
in the breaking of the bread.*

United Church of Christ Book of Worship

Michelangelo Merisi da Caravaggio, *Supper at Emmaus*

Diego Rodriguez de Silva y Velazquez, *The Moorish Kitchen Maid*

Velazquez focuses not on the table at Emmaus, but on the hidden girl working in the kitchen—listening, taking in the mysterious guest, the resurrected Christ.

The initiative in encounter belongs to the Lord.

But if we open the door of our being to him,

we shall share his life, his supper.

Gustavo Gutiérrez

ABUNDANT LIFE

Day by day, as they spent much time together in the temple, they broke bread at home and ate their food with glad and generous hearts, praising God and having the good will of all people.

Acts 2:46–47a

Luke presents us with an idealized moment in early Christian history.... We can learn much about life in the Christian community during the best of times. Notice that the life of faith was the passion of all the people remembered here. Indeed, faith focused the life of these people with one another, so that they gave themselves to what they had in common, not what distinguished them from one another. In this context, the members of the community accomplished great things that, in turn, brought a sense of awe to the whole community.

Marion Soards,
Thomas Dozeman, and
Kendall McCabe

Georg Gerster, *Coptic Church*

In regions of Ethiopia, Christian worship continues much as it has for hundreds of years, characterized by chanting, dancing, and drums.

Jacob Lawrence,
The Migration of the Negro

Lawrence's *Migration Series* deals
with the experience of African
Americans moving from the rural
South to the urban North.
One of the main forms of social
and recreational activity
in which the migrants indulged
occurred in the church.

A young father below me propped his bowed head on two fists stacked on a raised knee. The ushers and their trays vanished. The people had taken communion. No one moved. The organist hushed. All the men's heads were bent—black, white, red, yellow, and brown. The men sat absolutely still. Almost all the women's heads were bent, too, and some few tilted back. Some hats wagged faintly from side to side. All the people seemed scarcely to breathe. . . .

. . . Christ drifted among floating sandstone ledges and deep, absorbent skies. There was no speech nor language. The people had been praying, praying to God, just as they seem to be praying. That was the fact. I didn't know what to make of it.

Annie Dillard

Housewarming Blessing

Henry O. Tanner, *The Thankful Poor*

Our homes should be

places of security, safety, comfort,

hospitality, and humor.

They are places where we should

be able to be ourselves

. . . . Christian people will want

to affirm the presence of God

in their new home and

commit themselves to realizing

the divine presence in the spirit

and activities of the home.

Everyone gathers, if possible, in the hall of the house or flat or in the main room.

Leader: Early on a Sunday morning women discovered
that Jesus was risen. They were given a message
for his disciples . . . "He is gone before you
to Galilee." And he goes before us, too,
and is here to greet us, to welcome us as host.

A cross is placed in the middle of the hall or room.

All: Christ is here. God is with us.

Leader: This is the place for new beginnings,
but time past is a part of time present.
In the past lie causes of joy and sorrow.
Let us acknowledge the past with thankful hearts.

**All: This home is a place of welcome, a place
of celebration, a place of meeting, a place
of joy and sorrow, a place of rest and peace.**

Everyone moves to the kitchen.

Leader: What else will this home be?

**All: This home is a place of work,
the work of hands and head.**

Leader: What else is this house/flat?

**All: This is a part of the church,
the people of God.**

Everyone moves to the dining area.

Leader: What else is this home?

**All: This is a place for sharing—in worship,
in caring, in learning, in eating.**

Bread and wine are on the table.

Leader: Gracious God, we offer to you ourselves,
our minds and bodies, our home and
possessions, our strengths and weaknesses,
to share in the life and service of your [realm].
We ask your blessing on everyone and
everything that passes through this home.

All: Amen.

All share a meal.

Hazel Barkham

GOD'S OWN PEOPLE

But you are a chosen race,

a royal priesthood, a holy nation,

God's own people, in order

that you may proclaim the mighty

acts of the one who called

you out of the night into God's

marvelous light. Once you were

not a people, but now you are

God's people; once you had not

received mercy, but now you have

received mercy.

1 Peter 2:9–10

Arthur Boyd, *Moses Leading the People*

The words of 1 Peter 2 recall God's saving act, Moses and the Exodus. The covenant between God and the people established the Hebrews as God's own. The writer of First Peter identifies the church as a continuation of "the people of God."

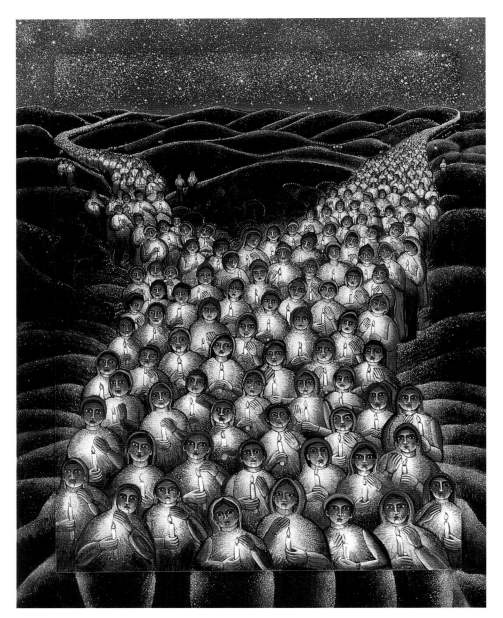

John August Swanson, *Festival of Lights*

MY PEOPLE

The night is beautiful,
So, the face of my people.

The stars are beautiful,
So the eyes of my people.

Beautiful, also, is the sun.
Beautiful, also are the souls of my people.

Langston Hughes

Peter and his followers assumed what we must struggle to accept, that the world will pass away. The great recurring theme of biblical narrative is always rescue, whether of Noah and his family, the people of Israel, or Christ's redeemed. The idea that there is a remnant too precious to be lost, in whom humanity will in some sense survive, has always been a generous hope, and a pious hope. For Peter this remnant is the ragtag community spreading into Rome and throughout its empire, the new Christians. Therefore in characterizing them to themselves he is describing those aspects of humanity dearest to God.

Marilyn Robinson

Eternal God,
we offer thanksgiving
and praise to you
on this festive day.
We give you thanks
for those who responded
to your call to establish
this church.

We acknowledge our
gratitude for the continuing
ministry and mission
of our church through
the years.
We thank you for all that
our church has meant to its
members, to those its
ministry has touched,
and to the United Church
of Christ.
In tender memory,
we rejoice at the inspiration
which has been found here,
through the preaching
of your word,
through the singing
of hymns to your praise,
and through the sharing
of life-sustaining sacraments.

Look upon us this day
with mercy.
Bless us as we reconsecrate
ourselves to you.
Sanctify our lives and our
work through this church.
Help us to preserve the best
of our past and to be open
to new vision.
May this local church long
continue to be a sign
of your Spirit and a witness
to Jesus Christ,
in whose name we pray.
Amen.

United Church of Christ Book of Worship

How baffling you are, oh Church,

and yet how I love you!

How you have made me suffer,

and yet how much I owe you!

I should like to see you destroyed,

and yet I need your presence.

You have given me so much scandal

and yet you have made me understand sanctity.

I have seen nothing in the world more

devoted to obscurity, more compromised,

more false, and I have touched nothing more pure,

more generous, more beautiful.

How often I have wanted to shut the doors

of my soul in your face, and how often

I have prayed to die in the safety of your arms.

No, I cannot free myself from you, because

I am you, although not completely.

And where should I go?

Carlo Carretto

Arthur Boyd,
Moses Leading the People, detail

Once you were not a people,
but now you are God's people.

BECAUSE I LIVE, YOU LIVE

Jesus said, "In a little while the world will no longer see me, but you will see me; because I live, you also will live. On that day you will know that I am in God, and you in me, and I in you."

John 14:19–20

How can we live and love as [Jesus] did, except through the mysterious gift and power which he gives through his Spirit, so that we become his face, his hands, his heart and body?

Jean Vanier

Emil Nolde, *Wildly Dancing Children*

Bagong Kussudiardja, *The Ascension*

The Indonesian artist celebrates the dancing Christ ascending to heaven. Christ lives; now we too may dance.

Whatever else the disciples would come to understand about

what had happened, they knew from the start that the resurrec-

tion was not simply about what happened to Jesus; it is about

victorious

what happens

to all who trust in Jesus, and about what can happen to all who

over death

claim this story as their own. The resurrection is not simply the

assurance that Jesus was victorious over death; it is also a

promise that we can share in that victory with him. The resur-

rection does not mean only that Jesus was triumphant over evil;

it also assures us that evil will not be ultimately triumphant in

our own lives. The resurrection is a promise offered to all. Saint

Jean Vianney said of Easter: "Today one grave is open, and from

it has risen a sun which will never be obscured, which will never

set, a sun which bestows new life."

Martin B. Copenhaver

Let the links of my shackles snap at every step
      of thy dance,
       O Lord of Dancing,
and let my heart wake in the freedom of the eternal voice.
Let it feel the touch of that foot that ever sets
      singing the lotus-seat of the muse,
and with its perfume maddens the air
      through ages.
Rebellious atoms are subdued into forms
      at thy dance time,
the suns and planets—anklets of light—twirl round
      thy moving feet,
and, age after age, things struggle to wake from
      dark slumber, through pain of life
      into consciousness,
and the ocean of thy bliss breaks out into tumults
      of suffering and joy.

Rabindranath Tagore

STEADFAST IN FAITH

Cast all your anxieties on God, because God cares for you.

1 Peter 5:7

What I expected was
Thunder, fighting,
Long struggles with men
And climbing.
After continual straining
I should grow strong;
the rocks would shake
And I should rest long.

What I had not foreseen
Was the gradual day
Weakening the will
Leaking the brightness away,
The lack of good to touch
The fading of body and soul
Like smoke before wind
Corrupt, unsubstantial.

...

For I had expected always
Some brightness to hold in trust,
Some final innocence
To save from dust;
That, hanging solid,
Would dangle through all
Like the created poem
Or the dazzling crystal.

Stephen Spender

Pablo Picasso, *Woman Crying*

Picasso painted this woman with intense, shocking colors and distorted forms to express her profound emotion.
He painted her emotions rather than her outward appearance.

George Tooker, *Girl Praying*

You are our protector,

You are our guardian and defender.

You are courage.

You are our haven and our hope.

You are our faith,

Our great consolation.

You are our eternal life,

Great and wonderful Lord,

God almighty,

Merciful Saviour.

St. Francis of Assisi

It is night.

The night is for stillness.
Let us be still in the presence of God.

It is night after a long day.
What has been done has been done;
what has not been done has not been done;
let it be.

The night is dark.
Let our fears of the darkness of the world and of our own lives
rest in you.

The night is quiet.
Let the quietness of your peace enfold us,
all dear to us,
and all who have no peace.

The night heralds the dawn.
Let us look expectantly to a new day,
new joys,
new possibilities.

In your name we pray.

amen

From "Night Prayer," in *A New Zealand Prayer Book*

Pentecost (CYCLE A)

Pentecost, in the *Rabbula Gospel*, detail

We savor the Pentecost moments—the ecstatic
experience of being released in the dance of the Spirit—
but we live in the steady gaze of the first disciples.

Red is the color of Pentecost Sunday—red flames of the Spirit uncontainable, filling and releasing the faithful at once, as the ecstatic dance of the American Indian Ghost Dancers filled and released them in hope. Yet the color of the season following Pentecost is green—the green of steady growth, of the most "ordinary time."

The church began in the passionate blaze of the Spirit, when boundaries of languages and cultures were transcended for a time and all heard the good news in their own language. The consuming fervor of the disciples communicated itself to all who encountered them and allowed for the remarkable spread of the Gospel throughout the known world.

Ecstasy is only part of the story, however. The work of living the Gospel depends more on sure, slow, steady, patient work—attentiveness, prayer, sacrifice, action. The eyes of the disciples in the mosaic of the sixth century *Rabbula Gospel* draw us in quietly, hold our attention, and point the way to a depth of commitment that is at the heart of a Gospel life.

We savor the Pentecost moments—the ecstatic experience of being released in the dance of the Spirit—but we live in the steady gaze of the first disciples, encouraging us to grow slowly, steadily deeper into an equally passionate commitment in the Spirit.

ECSTASY IS ONLY PART OF THE STORY

FILLED WITH THE SPIRIT

When the day of Pentecost had come, they were all together in one place. All of them were filled with the Holy Spirit and began to speak in other languages, as the Spirit gave them ability.

Acts 2:1, 4

As the Wind is your symbol, so forward our goings.
As the dove, so launch us heavenward.
As water, so purify our spirits.
As a cloud, so abate our temptations.
As dew, so revive our languor.
As fire, so purge out our dross. Amen.

Christina Rossetti

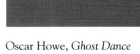

Oscar Howe, *Ghost Dance*

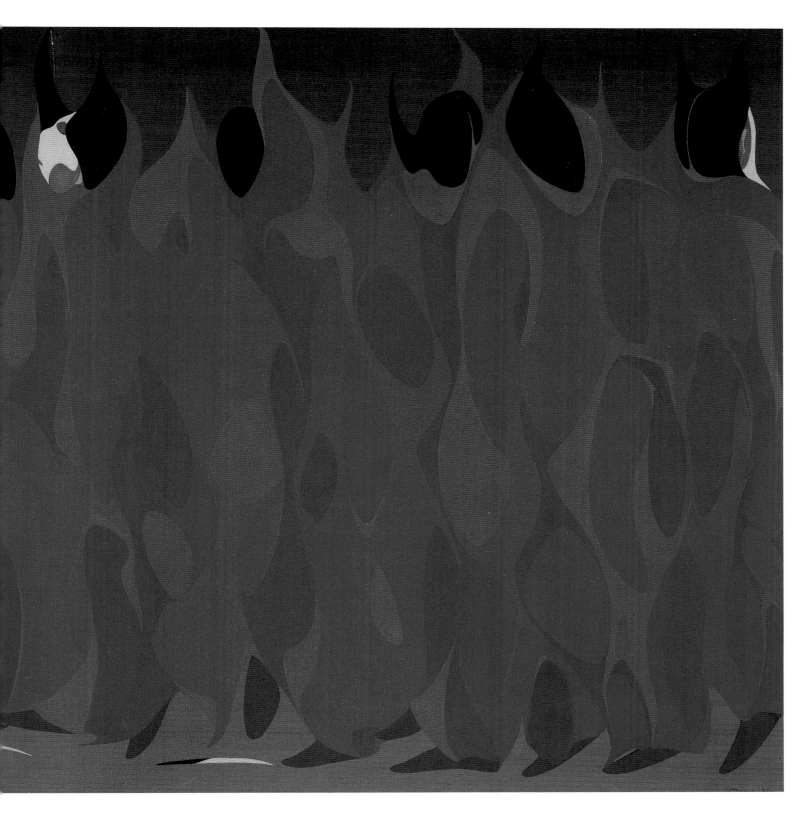

"Ghost Dancers," Indians of the North American West, were moved by the visions and spiritual hope of a nineteenth-century "crisis cult," which developed in response to their continuing displacement and oppression. Their hope was for the departure of the white settlers, and the restoration of their land and the buffalo. This abstract depiction renders the dancers' characteristic red coats as flames of passion and consummation.

Rabbula Gospel, *Pentecost*

Emotion in early Christian art is conveyed not through the action of the figures, but through their eyes. In the large eyes of Mary and the disciples can be seen the emotional impact of their Spirit-filled experience. The Virgin Mary and many of the disciples look directly at us as viewers, confronting us with their experience and perhaps inquiring about ours.

Veni Sancte Spiritus

Words: from the Pentecost Sequence;
Taizé Community, 1978

Music: Jacques Berthier, 1979

Come, Ho - ly Spir - it, from heav - en shine forth

with your glo - rious light. Ve - ni San - cte Spi - ri - tus.

Exuberant Spirit of God

Exuberant Spirit of God,
bursting with the brightness of flame
into the coldness of our lives
to warm us with a passion for justice and beauty,
we praise you.

Exuberant Spirit of God,
sweeping us out of the dusty corners of our apathy
to breathe vitality into our struggles for change,
we praise you.

Exuberant Spirit of God,
speaking words that leap over barriers of mistrust
to convey messages of truth and new understanding,
we praise you.

Exuberant Spirit of God,
flame
    wind
       speech,
burn, breathe, speak in us;
fill your world with justice and with joy.

Jan Berry

AND IT WAS GOOD

God saw everything

that God had made,

and indeed, it was

very good.

Genesis 1:31a

From *A Child's History of Hawaii*

This art by a Hawaiian child captures the moment
of creation separating light and dark, sea and dry land.

All you big things, bless the Lord
Mount Kilimanjaro and Lake Victoria
The Rift Valley and the Serengeti Plain
Fat baobabs and shady mango trees
All eucalyptus and tamarind trees
Bless the Lord
Praise and extol [God] for ever and ever.

All you tiny things, bless the Lord
Busy black ants and hopping fleas
Wriggling tadpoles and mosquito larvae
Flying locusts and water drops
Pollen dust and tsetse flies
Millet seeds and dried dagaa
Bless the Lord
Praise and extol [God] for ever and ever.

African Canticle

Bless the Lord, O my soul
Lord my God you are great
You are clothed with the energy of atoms
as with a mantle
From a cloud of whirling cosmic dust
as on the potter's wheel
you began to tease out the whorls of galaxies
and the gas escapes from your fingers condensing and burning
as you were fashioning the stars
You made a spatterdash of planets like spores or seeds
and scattered the comets like flowers. . . .

Ernesto Cardenal

O God eternal,
in your light I have seen
how closely you have conformed your creatures
to yourself.

I see that you have set us, as it were,
in a circle,
so that wherever we may go
we are still within this circle.

St. Catherine of Siena

216

Kenneth Noland, *Gift*

Bands of colors emanating from the center tease and delight the eye with a sense of creative movement and interaction and invite the viewer—"we are still within this circle."

YOU WILL BE A BLESSING

N ow God said to Abram, "Go from your country and your kindred and your parents' house to the land that I will show you. I will make of you a great nation, and I will bless you, and make your name great, so that you will be a blessing and in you all the families of the earth shall be blessed." So Abram went, as God had told him.

Genesis 12:1–2, 3b–4a

Jacopo Bassano, *Abraham's Journey*

The one who calls the worlds into being now makes a second call... addressed to aged Abraham and barren Sarah. The purpose... is to fashion an alternative community in creation gone awry, to embody in human history the power of the blessing.

Walter Brueggemann

John Mix Stanley, *Oregon City on the Willamette River*

Stanley highlights the implicit tension between the settlers and the indigenous inhabitants by placing the native couple at the margin of the painting and facing them toward the viewer. He thus requires engagement with their silent challenge.

[God], you have always mapped out
tomorrow's road:
and, although it is hidden,
today I believe.

Jeffery W. Rowthorn

The histories of the experience of indigenous peoples, evicted from their lands or even killed by settlers seeking a "promised land," caution us against reading this story of Abraham in a triumphant way. The full blessing of God to all the families of the earth has perhaps yet to be realized. It may await the time looked forward to by Robert Allen Warrior, an American Indian writer, when "the original inhabitants can become something other than subjects to be converted . . . or adversaries."

Blessed are you . . .

Creator of the universe, infinite and glorious,
you give us laws to save us from our folly;
give us eyes to see your plan unfolding,
your purpose emerging as the world is made;
give us courage to follow the truth,
courage to go where you lead;
then we shall know blessings beyond our dreams;
then will your will be done.

A New Zealand Prayer Book

Blessed are you,

God of growth and discovery;

yours is the inspiration

that has altered and changed our lives;

yours is the power that has brought us

to new dangers and opportunities.

Set us, your new creation,

to walk through this new world, watching and learning,

loving and trusting,

until your kingdom comes.

Amen

A New Zealand Prayer Book

O bless this people . . . who seek their own face
Under the mask and can hardly recognize it . . .

O bless this people. . . .

And with them, all the peoples of Europe,
All the peoples of Asia,
All the peoples of Africa,
All the peoples of America,
Who sweat blood and sufferings.

And see, in the midst of these millions of waves
The sea swell of the heads of my people.
And grant to their warm hands that they may clasp
The earth in a girdle of [loving] hands,
Beneath the rainbow of thy peace.

Leopold Sedar Senghor,
writing of the people of his country, Senegal

Abraham was a hundred years old when his son Isaac was born to him. Now Sarah said, "God has brought laughter for me; everyone who hears will laugh with me."

Genesis 21:5–6

It suddenly dawned on them that the wildest dreams they'd ever had hadn't been half wild enough.

Frederick Buechner

Rembrandt Harmensz van Rijn, *Abraham Entertaining the Three Angels*

Hiding at the door, Sarah, soon to laugh, eavesdrops on the visitors' news —
God's news — to Abraham: "Your wife shall have a son."

Magnificat

1

Now the fingers and toes are formed,
the doctor says.
Nothing to worry about. Nothing
to worry about

2

I will carry my belly to the mountain!
I will bare it to the moon, let the wolves howl,
I will wear it forever.
I will hold it up every morning in my ten fingers,
crowing
to wake the world.

3

This flutter that comes with me everywhere
is it my fear

or is it your jointed fingers
is it your feet

4

You are growing yourself
out   of   nothing:
there's   nothing
at last   I   can
do: I   stop
doing: you
are

5

Miles off in the dark,
my dark,
you head for dry land,

naked, safe
in salt waters.

Tides lap you.

Your breathing
makes me an ark.

Chana Bloch

SARAH

from *Sarah Laughed*

by Judy Gattis Smith

The following is taken

from a rhythmically

spoken piece for narrator,

two speaking choirs,

and a congregation

Rembrandt Harmensz van Rijn,
Abraham Entertaining the Three Angels, detail

Part 4

Old Sarah	Weak Sarah
Elderly	Ancient
Geriatric	Grey-haired
Wrinkled	Fading
Wasting	Weakening
Getting on in years	Over the hill

Yes!

She *shall* bear a son.

And Abraham fell on his face . . . and laughed!

Ha-ha *(continues)*
Ho-ho *(adding to above)*
Yuk-yuk *(adding to above)*

Part 5

Time went by. The Word came again

to Sarah	by three angels
behind a tent	out of sight

A child shall be *born!*

Part 6

And it began to bubble up . . .
that laugh again

She giggled	she shook
she tittered	she snickered
she chortled	she cackled
she crowed	she held her sides

She burst out *laughing!*

Ha-ha *(continues)*
Hee-hee *(adding to above)*
Ho-ho *(adding to above)*
Yuk-yuk *(adding to above)*

Part 7

Limp with laughter	rolling on the floor
rejoicing	delighted
exulting	jubilant
elated	flushed
whoopee	hurrah

huzzah-huzzah

yippee	yea rah
hosanna	hallelujah

hallel
Is anything too *wonderful* for God?

I meant to give you

a small surprise. . . .

Old people, as well

as young, must have

a little fun at times.

If I have frightened you,

I beg that you will

forgive me all the same.

Isak Dinesan

Ethan Hubbard, *Margaret Ovid at Church*,
Union Island, West Indies

From silly devotions and from sour-faced saints,

GOOD LORD,
DELIVER US!

Teresa of Avila

BAPTIZED INTO NEW LIFE

Therefore we have been buried

with Christ by baptism

into death, so that, just as Christ

was raised from the dead

by the glory of God, so we too

might walk in newness of life.

Romans 6:4

We awaken in Christ's body
as Christ awakens our bodies,
and my poor hand is Christ, He enters
my foot, and is infinitely me.

I move my hand, and wonderfully
my hand becomes Christ, becomes all of Him
(for God is indivisibly
whole, seamless in His Godhead).

I move my foot, and at once
He appears like a flash of lightning.
Do my words seem blasphemous?—Then
open your heart to Him

and let yourself receive the one
who is opening to you so deeply.
For if we genuinely love Him,
we wake up inside Christ's body

where all our body, all over,
every most hidden part of it,
is realized in joy as Him,
and He makes us, utterly, real,

and everything that is hurt, everything
that seemed to us dark, harsh, shameful,
maimed, ugly, irreparably
damaged, is in Him transformed

and recognized as whole, as lovely,
and radiant in His light
we awaken as the Beloved
in every last part of our body.

Symeon the New Theologian

Symeon the New Theologian, 949–1022, was a Greek Orthodox abbot, theologian, and poet. His discourses encouraged his monks to have a keen awareness of God's presence within them.

David Alan Harvey, *Baptism* (opposite)

Baptism is death which leads to life.

I am no longer afraid of death,
I know well
its dark, cold corridors
leading to life.

I am afraid rather of that life
which does not come out of death,
which cramps our hands
and slows our march.

Sometimes I wonder, in most
of our celebrations of baptism,
if we reduce the waters of
baptism to a mere sprinkle,
and cover it up with rosebuds
and lace and talk about cute
babies and "God loves you
and we love you" because we
dare not speak about the
strange and wonderful work
which is beginning in this
child on this day. You know
how we always try to avoid *death*.

Baptism is death which leads
to life.

William H. Willimon

I am afraid of my fear
and even more of the fear of others,
who do not know where they are going,
who continue clinging
to what they think is life
which we know to be death!

I live each day to kill death;
I die each day to give birth to life,
and in this death of death,
I die a thousand times
and am reborn another thousand
through that love
from my People,
which nourishes hope!

Julia Esquivel

Harriet Backer, *Baptism in Tanum Church*, 1892

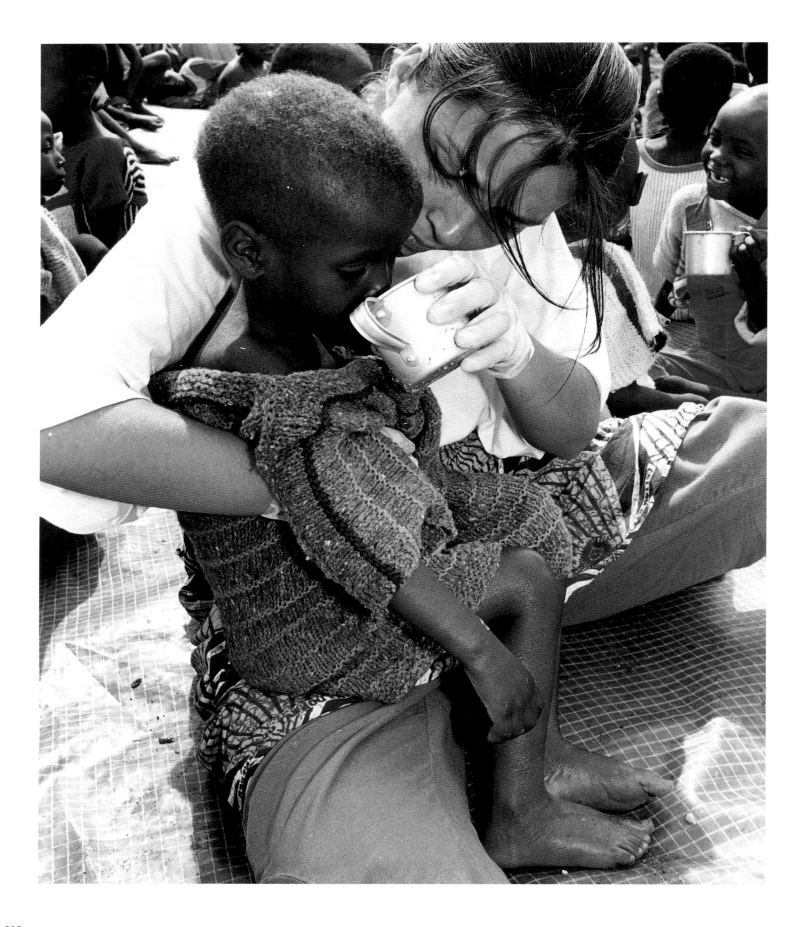

EVEN A CUP OF COLD WATER

jesus said, "Whoever welcomes you welcomes me, and whoever welcomes me welcomes the one who sent me, and whoever gives even a cup of cold water to one of these little ones in the name of a disciple—truly I tell you, none of these will lose their reward."

Matthew 10:40, 42

It is worth some reflection to try to discern the patterns of this self-maintaining cycle of human suffering. For a person who feels unvalued, unappreciated, and goalless is not capable of generosity and appreciation of others and therefore, not capable of empathy and concern with their hunger and their need. In the strictest sense, such a person needs to be rescued, redeemed, or saved as much as the starving person whose quality of life is shriveled and brutalized needs to be rescued, redeemed, or saved. Both are living a life that is unfree, less than human, and marred by needless suffering. But the fearful frustration and torture of the physically starving person can only be resolved by that redemption of the love-starved which consists of a radical conversion from self-centeredness to engagement with and for others.

Monika Hellwig

John Hopper, *Rwandan Starving Children* (opposite)

A story said to originate
in a Russian Orthodox monastery
has an older monk
telling a younger one:
"I have finally learned to
accept people as they are.
Whatever they are in the world,
a prostitute, a prime minister,
it is all the same to me.
But sometimes I see a stranger
coming up the road and I say,
'Oh, Jesus Christ, is it you again?' "

Kathleen Norris

Andrei Rublev, *Icon of the Trinity*

The image of the three heavenly visitors at the table is based on the story in Genesis of their appearance to Abraham and Sarah. The hosts greet the mysterious guests with utmost hospitality. They discover only later that they have been entertaining messengers of God. The Eastern church often interprets this image of the visitors as an image of the Trinity, in relationship with one another and to the world, symbolized by the meal they share.

Walking up the damp hill in the hot sun, there were signs of the recent heavy rains. The land smelled fresh, shaded plants still held moisture in their green clustered leaves, and fresh deer tracks pointed uphill like arrows in the dark, moist soil.

Along our way, my friend and I stopped at a cluster of large boulders to drink fresh rain collected in a hollow bowl that had been worn into stone over slow centuries. Bending over the stone, smelling earth up close, we drank sky off the surface of water. Mosses and ancient lichens lived there. And swimming in another stone cup were slender orange newts, alive and vibrant with the rains.

Drinking the water, I thought how earth and sky are generous with their gifts and how good it is to receive them. Most of us are taught, somehow, about giving and accepting human gifts, but not about opening ourselves and our bodies to welcome the sun, the land, the visions of sky and dreaming, not about standing in the rain ecstatic with what is offered.

Linda Hogan

I saw a stranger yestereen:
I put food in the eating place,
drink in the drinking place,
music in the listening place;
and in the blessed name of the Triune
he blessed myself and my house,
my cattle and my dear ones,
and the lark said in her song
    often, often, often,
goes the Christ in the stranger's guise
    often, often, often,
goes the Christ in the stranger's guise.

Old Gaelic Rune

Hospitality is one form of worship.

Jewish Proverb

I WILL GIVE YOU REST

Come to me, all you that are weary

and are carrying heavy burdens,

and I will give you rest. Take my yoke

upon you, and learn from me;

for I am gentle and humble in heart,

and you will find rest for your souls.

For my yoke is easy, and my

burden is light.

Matthew 11:28–30

The "rest" Jesus promises summons up the image of the eschatological rest in the days of the Messiah, of which the sabbath rest was a symbol and a foretaste. Paradoxically, Jesus' "rest" was also a kind of "yoke," a symbol used by the rabbis for the Mosaic law. . . . Central to the yoke or law of Jesus. . . . is Jesus himself. . . . The spiritual rest Jesus gives comes from assimilating and living Jesus' attitudes, indeed, his very person.

John P. Meier

Henry Moore, *Memorial Figure*

The paradox of the "easy yoke" and "light burden" seems to be echoed in Moore's *Memorial Figure*, where Moore shapes the great mass of stone into an image at once graceful, fluid, and serene.

Now I lay me down to sleep,
I pray thee, God, thy child to keep;
Thy love go with me all the night,
and wake me with the morning light.

Traditional English Child's Evening Prayer

I WILL GIVE YOU REST.

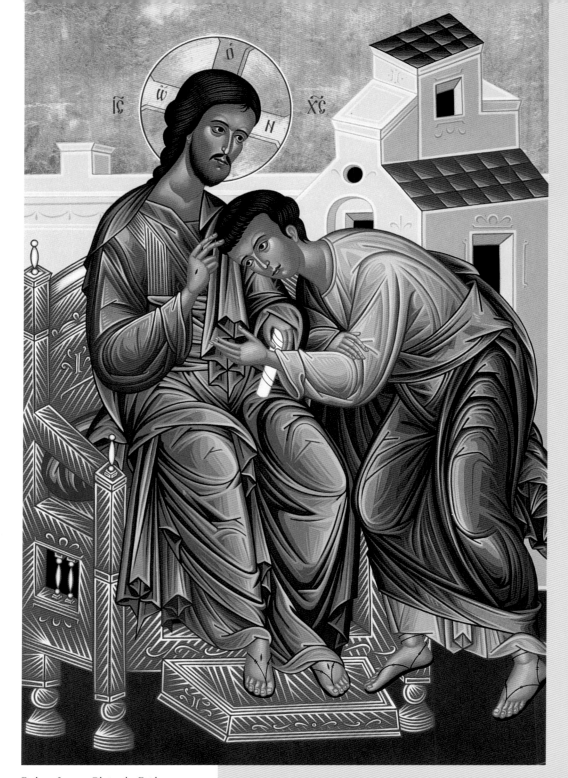

Robert Lentz, *Christ the Bridegroom*

At the table of the last supper,
one of his disciples—the one whom Jesus loved—
was reclining next to him.

John 13:23

Come Unto Me

A Eucharistic Prayer Based on Matthew 11 and Wisdom Texts (Excerpts)

People: For Wisdom is true to her name.
Put your feet into her fetters,
and your neck into her collar;
Offer your shoulder to her burden,
do not be impatient of her bonds.

Leader: Court her with all your soul,
and with all your might keep in her ways;
search for her, track her down: she will reveal
herself; once you hold her, do not let her go.

People: For in the end you will find rest in her
and she will take the form of joy for you:
her fetters you will find a mighty defense,
Her yoke will be a golden ornament.
(Ecclesiastes 6:22a, 23–30)

Leader: Jesus said, "Come unto me, all you who
labor and are overburdened, and I will give you rest; shoulder
my yoke and learn from me, for I am gentle and humble in
heart, and you will find rest for your souls.

People: "Yes, my yoke is easy and my burden is light."
(Matthew 11:28, 29)

Susan Cady, Marian Ronan, Hal Taussig

The Lone, Wild Bird

The lone, wild bird, in lofty flight,
Is still with Thee, nor leaves Thy sight.
And I am Thine! I rest in Thee.
Great Spirit come, and rest in me.
The ends of earth are in Thy hand,
The sea's dark deep and far-off land.
And I am Thine, I rest in Thee!
Great Spirit come, and rest in me.

Henry Richard McFadyen

A SOWER WENT OUT TO SOW

And Jesus told them

many things

in parables, saying:

"Listen! A sower

went out to sow."

Matthew 13:3

Christ told his parables in terms of things that never change in the barest fundamentals of living. And we can claim them for our own if we will make the effort to pierce the years with a little study, to breathe the clean air of the countryside and lift our eyes to the stars. . . . In a city park in London, in the sprawling mechanized farms of the American Middle West, in a backyard garden of a window box there is still a seed and a sower.

April Oursler Armstrong

Vincent van Gogh, *The Sower*

Betsy James, *Double Spiral*

Living Hearts

Sower of living hearts,
sower of tenderness,
sower of courage,
sower of service,
sower of prayer,
sower of light.
Lord,
sow within us!

Sower of gifts,
sower of forgiveness,
sower of faith,
sower of joy,
sower of life,
sower of the Beatitudes.
Lord, sow
in the hearts of all people!

Even if we are hard
as stones,
be patient with us!
Your Good News
will manage to slip
between the tight cracks
in our rock and will
grow into giant sheaves
of Good News!

Charles Singer and Albert Hari

O God, sow within us!

Vincent van Gogh, *Wheat Field with Crows*

One summer that stood out as hot and dry, above all other hot and dry summers . . . many settlers were forced to walk away, back to where they had come from, leaving their farms and their vigor and their excuse for living behind with their bills. . . .

The ponds had been crusty and cracked since April, except for the big one where we had put the well and windmill, close to the road. There we had one mesquite tree twenty feet high. The shade below was sketchy, but it was one point scored against an all-consuming sun.

Katie Breeze

God's dominion is a "process."
Like seed that has
germinated, its potential
for growth is a function
of the collaboration
of God's activity and
human response . . .
a process of growth
and the nature of the yield.

Paul Hammer

WHEAT OR WEEDS?

Let both the wheat and weeds grow together until the harvest; and at harvest time I will tell the reapers, Collect the weeds first and bind them in bundles to be burned, but gather the wheat into my barn.

Matthew 13:30

Patrick DesJarlait,
Gathering Wild Rice

Up until the *parousia*, the church will always be a mixed bag of good and evil; it should not play God by trying to justify itself completely through purges and Inquisitions. . . . The definitive separation must be left to the last judgment; it is the church's part to preach repentance and practice patience.

John P. Meier

Soichi Sunami, *Martha Graham and Group in "Heretic"*

Society's tendency to isolate, ostracize, and judge is choreographed in Martha Graham's dance "Heretic."

Mr. Head stood very still and felt the action of mercy touch him again but this time he knew that there were no words in the world that could name it. He understood that it grew out of agony, which is not denied to any man and which is given in strange ways to children. He understood it was all a man could carry into death to give his Maker and he suddenly burned with shame that he had so little of it to take with him. He stood appalled, judging himself with the thoroughness of God, while the action of mercy covered his pride like a flame and consumed it. He had never thought himself a great sinner before but he saw now that his true depravity had been hidden from him lest it cause him despair. He realized that he was for-given for sins from the beginning of time, when he had conceived in his own heart the sin of Adam, until the present, when he had denied poor Nelson. He saw that no sin was too mon-strous for him to claim as his own, and since God loved in proportion as [God] forgave, he felt ready at that instant to enter Paradise.

Flannery O'Connor

For the hungry and the overfed,
May we have enough.

For the mourners and the mockers,
May we laugh together.

For the victims and the oppressors,
May we share power wisely.

For the peacemakers and the warmongers,
May clear truth and stern love lead us to harmony.

For the silenced and the propagandists,
May we speak our own words in truth.

For the unemployed and the overworked,
May our impress on the earth be kindly and creative.

For the troubled and the sleek,
May we live together as wounded healers.

For the homeless and the cosseted,
May our homes be simple, warm and welcoming.

For the vibrant and the dying,
May we all die to live.

From "Midday Prayer," *A New Zealand Prayer Book*

Yet I shall temper so Justice with mercy.

John Milton

P A R A B L E S   O F   G O D ' S   D O M I N I O N

✝he dominion of heaven is like . . .

Matthew 13:33a

"The dominion of heaven is like
a mustard seed that someone took
and sowed in a field; it is the
smallest of all the seed, but when it
has grown it is the greatest of
shrubs and becomes a tree,
so that the birds of the air come
and make nests in its branches."

Matthew 13:31–32

Suzanne Marshall, *Journey Through Time*

God longs for God
and uses us,
rises in us . . .
becomes in us.
Let us be silent,
a quiet dough

where God moves
into every pore . . .
where God lives
as God pleases.

Let us rise simply,
a quiet dough.

Gunilla Norris

"The dominion of heaven is like
yeast that a woman took and mixed
in with three measures of flour
until all of it was leavened."

Matthew 13:33

. . . But we who will eat the bread when we come in
Out of the cold and dark know it is a deeper mystery
That brings the bread to rise:

it is the love and faith
Of large and lonely women, moving like floury clouds
In farmhouse kitchens, that rounds the loaves and the lives
Of those around them . . .
Just as we know it is hunger—
Our own and others'—that gives all salt and savor to bread. . . .

Thomas McGrath

The dominion of heaven is like . . .

"Again, the dominion of heaven is like a merchant in search of fine pearls; on finding one pearl of great value, he went and sold all that he had and bought it."

Matthew 13:45

A condition of complete simplicity

(Costing not less than everything)

And all shall be well and

all manner of things shall be well.

T. S. Eliot

Jan Vermeer, *Woman Holding a Balance*

Bathed in soft light, this prosperous woman weighs her pearl. Behind her on the wall is a painting of the Last Judgment. Among the wealthiest people of the world in the seventeenth century, the Dutch were also quite religious. The painting depicts their valuing of the material while perhaps suggesting that such riches are fleeting.

Field of Vision

I remember this woman who sat for years
in a wheelchair, looking straight ahead
Out the window at sycamore trees unleafing
and leafing at the far end of the lane.

Straight out past the TV in the corner,
The stunted, agitated hawthorne bush,
The same small calves with their backs to wind and rain,
The same acre of ragwort, the same mountain.

She was steadfast as the big window itself.
Her brow as clear as the chrome bits of the chair.
She never lamented once and she never
Carried a spare ounce of emotional weight.

Face to face with her was an education
Of the sort you got across a well-braced gate—
One of those lean, clean, iron, roadside ones
Between two whitewashed pillars, where you could see

Deeper into the country than you expected
And discovered that the field behind the hedge
Grew more distinctly strange as you kept standing
Focused and drawn in by what barred the way.

Seamus Heaney

Again, the dominion of heaven
is like a net that was thrown into the sea
and caught fish of every kind."

Matthew 13:47

"The dominion of heaven is like
a treasure hidden in a field. "

Matthew 13:44

Forbear to judge, for we are sinners all.
Close up his eyes, and draw the curtain close;
And let us all to meditation.

William Shakespeare

Jacopo Bassano, *The Miraculous Draught of Fishes*

"Have you understood all this?" They answered, "Yes." And he said to them,

"Therefore every scribe who has been trained for the dominion of heaven
is like the head of a household who brings out of his treasure what is new and what is old."

Matthew 13:51–52

FACE TO FACE ENCOUNTER

Jacob was left alone; and a man wrestled with him until daybreak. So Jacob called the place Peniel, saying, "For I have seen God face to face and yet my life is preserved."

Genesis 32:24, 30

COME, O THOU TRAVELER UNKNOWN

Come, O thou Traveler unknown,
   Whom I still hold, but cannot see;
My company before is gone,
   And I am left alone with thee,
With thee all night I mean to stay,
And wrestle till the break of day.

In vain thou strugglest to get free,
   I never will unloose my hold:
Art thou the [One] that died for me?
   The secret of thy love unfold.
Wrestling I will not let thee go,
Till I thy name, thy nature show.

Yield to me now,—for I am weak;
   But confident in self-despair:
Speak to my heart, in blessings speak,
   Be conquered by my instant prayer,
Speak, or thou never hence shall move,
And tell me if thy name is Love.

My prayer hath power with God; the Grace
   Unspeakable I now receive,
Through Faith I see thee face to face,
   I see thee face to face, and live:
In vain I have not wept, and strove,
Thy nature and thy name is Love.

Charles Wesley

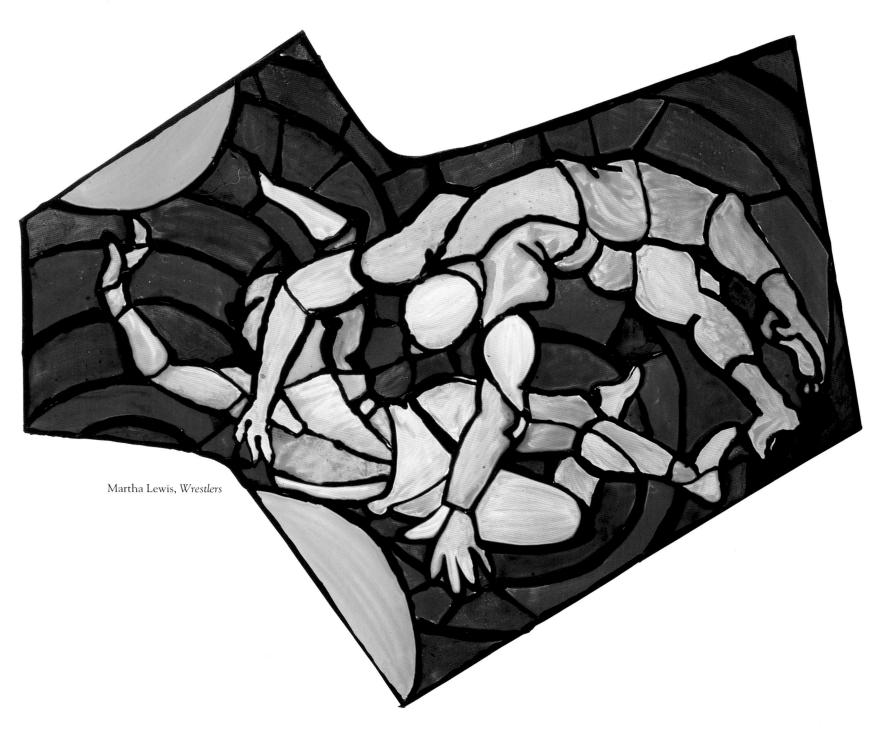

Martha Lewis, *Wrestlers*

Both were wounded: Jacob at the hip, the angel in his vanity. Yet they parted friends, or was it accomplices? Jacob accepted his aggressor's departure willingly; the latter, as if to thank him, made him a gift: a new name which for generations to come would symbolize eternal struggle and endurance, in more than one land, during more than one night.

At dawn Jacob was a different man. Whatever he touched caught fire. His words acquired a new resonance; he now expressed himself as a visionary, a poet.

Elie Wiesel

Paul Gauguin, *Vision After the Sermon (Jacob Wrestling the Angel)*

Gauguin has split this image with a tree limb, dividing the pious Breton peasants from their vision of Jacob wrestling the angel.

It's Me in That Struggle

What struck me about that story at that time [of great family turmoil] was that Jacob was wounded wrestling with God and in the process all the names that had worked before left him and he was given a new one. That was what was happening to me. I felt terribly wounded, and all the neat categories that had ordered my existence to that point dissolved, and I was faced with chaos. I was in desperate need of new names, and although I longed to do it, I couldn't take a few weeks off, flee to some place of retreat to confront what I was going through and there discover the new order, and be given the new names. I had to come up with the new names there and then, in the midst of getting the boys off to school, working at Union Seminary, visiting Peggy in the hospital, trying to find ways of talking about illness to a six year old, doing the dishes, shopping for school clothes, picking up at birthday parties, talking endlessly to everyone, exhausted. . . . And I needed the names,—because I was anxious, frightened, bitter, and angry, badly wounded and limping.

Linda Clark

I had a book of Bible stories when I was a kid. There was a picture I'd look at twenty times every day: Jacob wrestles with the angel. I don't really remember the story, or why the wrestling—just the picture. Jacob is young and very strong. The angel is a . . . beautiful man, with golden hair and wings, of course. I still dream about it. Many nights. I'm . . . It's me. In that struggle. Fierce, and unfair. The angel is not human, and it holds nothing back, so could anyone human win, what kind of a fight is it? It's not just. Losing means your soul thrown down in the dust, your heart torn out from God's. But you can't not lose.

Joe in the drama *Angels in America, Part One: Millennium Approaches* by Tony Kushner

May we realize that God's blessing upon us—that for which we have wrestled, some of us for so long and so fiercely—is that we be empowered to welcome and bless those who, like Jacob, indeed, like most of us, do not deserve to be blessed.

May we sustain the confidence and courage, the compassion and humor, to realize the sacred power in this stunning opportunity which is ours today, and will be ours, forever.

This blessing will not be taken from us.

Carter Heyward

YOU OF LITTLE FAITH

J esus said, "Come." So Peter got out of the boat, started walking on the water, and came toward Jesus. But when he noticed the strong wind, he became frightened, and beginning to sink cried out, "Lord, save me!" Jesus immediately reached out his hand and caught Peter saying to him, "You of little faith, why did you doubt?"

Matthew 14:29–31

Jesus' miracle of walking on the sea is not just to "show off" who he is but to come to the aid of his threatened disciples. That is to say, while the story is indeed talking about who Jesus is, it emphasizes his *function* rather than his *nature*. As Messiah he is the one charged and empowered by God to shepherd and care for God's people.

Douglas R. A. Hare

Comfortless, helpless, and forsaken, we are altogether undone. O God, thou wilt not leave our hope. Martin Luther

Winslow Homer, *On a Lee Shore* (opposite)

Henry O. Tanner, *Christ Walking on Water*

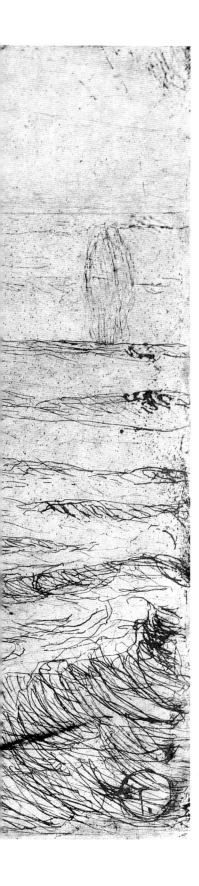

Give me to be in Your presence,
God, even though I know it
only as absence.

May Sarton

 Lord Jesus our God

Who called people from their daily work

Saying to them, "Come ye after me,"

May your children today hear your voice

And gladly answer your call

To give their lives to you

To serve your Church

And give their hearts

To you only.

Bless their hopes

The first tiny stirrings of desire

The little resolve to go forward

The small vision of what might be.

Deal gently with their fears

The hesitation of uncertainty

The darkness of the unknown

The lack of confidence in their own capacity

And turn it all to trust in you.

Gabrielle Hadington

To be joyful out on
70,000 fathoms of water,
many, many miles from
all human help—yes,
that is something great!
To swim in the shallows
in the company of waders
is not the religious.

Sören Kierkegaard

. . . the religious contradiction: simultaneously to be out on
70,000 fathoms of water and yet be joyful.

Sören Kierkegaard

How very good and pleasant it is

when kindred live together in unity!

Psalm 133:1

Alone you stood before God when [God] called you; alone you had to answer that call; alone you had to struggle and pray; and alone you will die and give an account to God. You cannot escape from yourself; for God has singled you out. If you refuse to be alone you are rejecting Christ's call to you, and you can have no part in the community of those who are called. . . . But the reverse is also true: let those who are not in community beware of being alone. Into the community you were called, the call was not meant for you alone; in the community of the called you bear your cross, you struggle, you pray.

Dietrich Bonhoeffer

Palmer Hayden, *Midsummer Night in Harlem*

I must give the people around me credit for encouraging me for doing the right thing in the right way. I don't know what would have happened if they had said, "That's not the way to do it." . . . In retrospect [Harlem] was a great community; it was a very fascinating community. If you had asked me this forty years ago, I wouldn't have used these terms. . . . It was a very cohesive community. You knew people. You didn't know their names, but you'd pass people on the street and see the face over and over again. . . . You knew the police, you knew the firemen, you knew the teachers, the people on the street. You knew the peddlar. It was *me*.

Jacob Lawrence

Within the mural:

BEHOLD, HOW GOOD AND HOW PLEASANT IT IS FOR BRETHREN TO DWELL TOGETHER IN UNITY!
IT IS LIKE
THE PRECIOUS
OINTMENT
UPON THE HEAD...
AS THE DEW
OF HERMON
AND AS THE DEW
THAT DESCENDED
UPON THE MOUNTAINS
OF ZION:
FOR THERE THE LORD
COMMANDED
THE BLESSING
EVEN LIFE
FOR EVERMORE.

Ben Shahn,
Mosaic mural at
LeMoyne-Owens College

Into the community you were

God of all, source and goal of community,
whose will is that all your people enjoy
fullness of life, may we be builders
of community, caring for your good earth
here and worldwide, that we may delight
in diversity and choose solidarity, for you are
in community with us, our God, forever.

Amen.

Anonymous

Hine Ma Tov
(How Very Good and Pleasant It Is)

Words: Psalm 133:1

Music: Israeli round

called...

To sing this as a round, divide into two groups. Groups A sings Part 1 twice,
then Part 2 twice. Group B sings Part 1 as Group A sings Part 2.

WE, WHO ARE MANY—ONE BODY

We, who are many, are one body in Christ, and individually we are members one of another.

Romans 12:5

L'Arche, however, is built not on words, but on the body. The community of L'Arche is a community formed around the wounded bodies of handicapped people. Feeding, cleaning, touching, holding—this is what builds the community. Words are secondary. Most handicapped people have few words to speak, and many do not speak at all. It is the language of body that counts most.

"The word became flesh." That is the center of the Christian message. Often the body was seen as a hindrance to the full realization of what the word wanted to express. But Jesus confronts us with the word that can be seen, heard, and touched. The body thus becomes the way to know the word and to enter into relationship with the word. The body of Jesus becomes the way of life.

Henri J. Nouwen

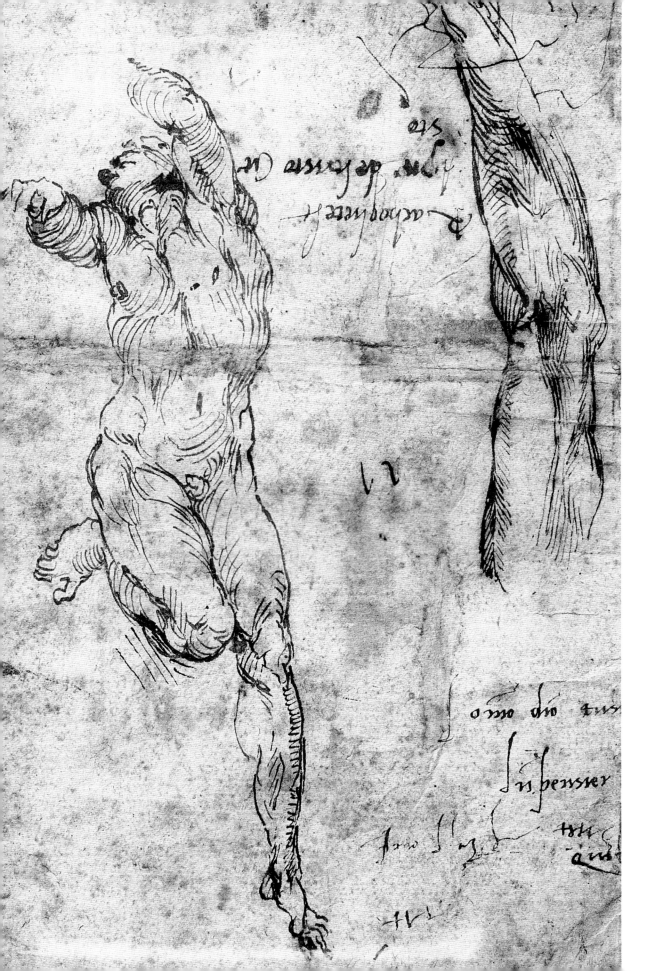

Michelangelo Buonarotti,
Study of St. Sebastian

Many Gifts,
One Spirit

If there were not diversity in the body, and all members were the same or nearly the same, the body would be a nearly unrecognizable, nonfunctional entity.

Clarice Martin

Because I am a Christian and because I think my own family of faith needs to learn inclusiveness perhaps more than any other, I must now utilize specifically Christian terminology. It is my conviction that . . . a conscious cooperation infused with the Holy Spirit calls us toward an all-inclusive attitude, a theology of the wind, a relationship to God and the world that does not try to make things easy by ruling out whole areas of human experience and whole groups of human beings. . . . Some women and other minority people have begun to clamor for first-class citizenship, church members may rejoice that we are being offered the opportunity to move toward wholeness—not just the wholeness of Christ's body, the church, but also our own internal wholeness.

Hildegard of Bingen,
All Creatures Celebrate
(opposite)

Virginia Mollenkott

Many gifts, one Spirit, one love known in many ways.
In our difference is blessing, from diversity we praise,
one Giver, one Lord, one Spirit, one Word
known in many ways, hallowing our days,
for the Giver, for the gifts, praise, praise, praise!

God of change and glory, God of time and space,
when we fear the future, give to us your grace.
In the midst of changing ways, give us still the grace to praise.

God of many colors, God of many signs,
you have made us different, blessing many kinds.
As the old ways disappear, let your love cast out our fear.

Freshness of the morning, newness of each night,
you are still creating endless love and light.
This we see, as shadows part, many gifts from one great heart.

Al Carmines

Text Sources

Foreword

John Gilmour, *Picturing the World* (Albany: State University of New York Press, 1986), 22.

Praying and Imaging: The Art of Contemplation

Henri J. M. Nouwen, *Behold the Beauty of the Lord: Praying with Icons* (Notre Dame, Ind.: Ave Maria Press, 1991), 12.

Edward Robinson, *The Language of Mystery* (Philadelphia: Trinity Press International, 1987), 33.

Proper 17 (Pentecost 13)

"We're Gonna Sit at the Welcome Table," traditional spiritual.

George Herbert, "Love Bade Me Welcome," from *Five Mystical Songs*, distributed in the U.S. by Galaxy Music Corp.

Joetta Handrich Schlabach, *Extending the Table: A World Community Cookbook* (Scottdale, Pa.: Herald Press, 1991), 18. Used by permission.

Elsa Tamez, "Feast of Life," in *International Review of Mission*, 1982.

Proper 18 (Pentecost 14)

Madeleine L'Engle, *Anytime Prayers* (Wheaton, Ill.: Harold Shaw, 1994), 52. © Crosswicks, 1994. Used by permission.

Nanao Sakaki, "Just Enough," in *Break the Mirror* (New York: Farrar, Straus & Giroux, 1987). Copyright © 1987 by Nanao Sakaki. Used by permission of North Point Press, a division of Farrar, Straus & Giroux, Inc.

Proper 19 (Pentecost 15)

Ntozake Shange, "a laying on of hands," in *A Choreopoem: For Colored Girls Who Have Considered Suicide/When the Rainbow Is Enuf* (New York: Collier, 1977), 60–63. Used by permission of Simon & Schuster, Inc.

Adrienne Rich, from "Upper Broadway," in *The Dream of a Common Language: Poems 1974–77* (New York: Norton, 1978), 41. Copyright © 1978 by W. W. Norton & Company, Inc. Used by permission of the author and W. W. Norton & Company, Inc.

Lal Ded, "I Was Passionate," trans. Colman Barks, in *Women in Praise of the Sacred*, ed. Jane Hirshfield (New York: HarperCollins, 1994), 120. Used by permission.

Proper 20 (Pentecost 16)

"Guernika," in *The Civil War in Spain, 1936–1939*, ed. Robert Payne (New York: Putnam, 1962), 195–97, quoted in Alberto de Onaindía, "Guernica Aflame," *Picasso's Guernica*, ed. Ellen Oppler (New York: Norton, 1988), 163–64.

Janet Morley, "Holy God," in *Bread of Tomorrow: Prayers for the Church Year*, ed. Janet Morley (Maryknoll, N.Y.: Orbis Books; London: Christian Aid, 1992), 89–91. Used by permission.

"There Is a Balm in Gilead," African American spiritual, in *The New Century Hymnal* (Cleveland: Pilgrim Press, 1995).

Proper 21 (Pentecost 17)

Erasmus, *The Enchridian of Erasmus*, trans. and ed. Raymond Himelick (Bloomington, Ind.: Indiana University Press, 1963), 57. Used by permission.

Dietrich Bonhoeffer, *The Cost of Discipleship* (New York: Macmillan, 1963), 57.

Ada María Isasi-Díaz, "A Hispanic Garden in a Foreign Land," in *Inheriting Our Mothers' Gardens: Feminist Theology in Third World Perspective*, ed. Katie Geneva Canon et al. (Philadelphia: Westminster, 1988), 99. Used by permission.

J. S. Bach, "Cantata BWV 147," libretto by Salomon Franck, trans. Lionel Salter (New York: Deutsche Grammophon, 1992).

Dag Hammarskjöld, *Markings*, trans. Leif Sjoberg and W. H. Auden (New York: Alfred A. Knopf, 1966), 214–15. Translation © 1964 by Alfred A. Knopf, Inc., and Faber & Faber Ltd. Used by permission.

Proper 22 (Pentecost 18)

Marie Livingston Roy, "The Legacy," *Accent on Youth*, vol. 17, no. 1 (Fall 1984), 3. Used by permission.

Sister Ann Patrick Ware, Women's Liturgy Group of New York, 100 LaSalle Street, New York, NY 10027. This text may be used or republished by any reader without further authorization from any party.

"A Song of Greatness: A Chippewa Indian Song," trans. Mary Austin, in *My Song Is Beautiful: Poems and Pictures in Many Voices*, selected by Mary Ann Hoberman (Boston: Little, Brown, 1994), 15. Used by permission of Houghton Mifflin Company.

Carl R. Holladay, "II Timothy 1:1–14," in Fred B. Craddock et al., *Preaching through the Christian Year: A* (Philadelphia: Trinity Press International, 1992), 191.

Proper 23 (Pentecost 19)

Denise Dombkowski Hopkins, *Journey Through the Psalms: A Path to Wholeness* (New York: United Church Press, 1990).

Paul Hammer, "The Background Word," in *Word Among Us: A Worship-centered, Lectionary-based Curriculum for the Whole Congregation* Leader's Guides (Cleveland: United Church Press, 1995), Proper 23. Used by permission.

Francis of Assisi, "Canticle of the Sun," adapted.

Joseph R. Renville, "Wakantanka Taku Nitawa (Many and Great, O God, Are Your Works)," paraphrased by R. Philip Frazier in *The New Century Hymnal* (Cleveland: Pilgrim Press, 1995).

Proper 24 (Pentecost 20)

Eudora Welty, *The Collected Stories of Eudora Welty* (New York: Harcourt Brace Jovanovich, 1980), 154.

Walt Whitman, *An American Primer*, ed. Horace Traubel (1904), abridged and reprinted in *Parabola: Magazine of Myth and Tradition*, vol. 8, no. 3 (August 3, 1993): 6.

Anderson Clark, unpublished letters. Used by permission.

Harold Kushner, *Questions of Faith: Contemporary Thinkers Respond*, ed. Dolly Patterson (Philadelphia: Trinity Press International, 1990), 64. Used by permission.

Proper 25 (Pentecost 21)

Brian Wren, "What Language Shall I Borrow?" in *God-Talk in Worship: A Male Response to Feminist Theology* (New York: Crossroad, 1984), 205. Used by permission.

Hildegard of Bingen, "Antiphon for the Holy Spirit I," in *Hildegard of Bingen: Mystical Writing*, ed. and introduced by Fiona Bowie and Oliver Davies (New York: Crossroad, 1990), 118. Used by permission.

Mary Batchelor, *Opening Up the Bible* (Oxford, England: Lion, 1993), 65.

"Glory to You, Almighty God," in *A Wee Worship Book* (Glasgow, Scotland: Iona Community, 1988). Used by permission.

All Saints' Day

Dag Hammarskjöld, *Markings*, trans. Leif Sjoberg and W. H. Auden (New York: Alfred A. Knopf, 1966), 84. Translation © 1964 by Alfred A. Knopf, Inc., and Faber & Faber Ltd. Used by permission.

Stephen Spender, "I Think Continually of Those Who Were Truly Great," in *Modern Religious Poems*, ed. Jacob Trapp (New York: Harper & Row, 1964), 166. Used by permission of Faber & Faber.

"Invocation of the Saints," from *The Covenant of Peace: A Liberation Prayer Book*, in *The Wideness of God's Mercy: Litanies to Enlarge Our Prayer*, ed. Jeffery W. Rowthorn (Minneapolis: Seabury Press, 1985), 135–37. Used by permission of John Pairman Brown.

Proper 26 (Pentecost 22)

Paul Laurence Dunbar, "We Wear the Mask," in *The Complete Poems of Paul Laurence Dunbar* (New York: Dodd, Mead & Co., 1913), 71.

Miriam Therese Winter, "Zacchaeus," in *Joy Is Like the Rain* (Hartford, Conn.: Medical Mission Sisters, 1965). Used by permission.

Fred Craddock, *Luke* (Louisville: John Knox, 1990), 219.

Sara M. deHall, "Si Fui Motivo de Dolor, Oh Dios (If I Have Been the Source of Pain, O God)," based on text by C. M. Battersby, trans. Janet W. May, in *The New Century Hymnal* (Cleveland: Pilgrim Press, 1995). English translation Copyright ©1992 United Church Board for Homeland Ministries/Pilgrim Press, Cleveland, Ohio. Used by permission.

Proper 27 (Pentecost 23)

Victor Hugo, "Be Like the Bird," in *The Illustrated Treasury of Children's Literature* (New York: Grossett and Dunlap, 1955), 133.

James Agee, from "Knoxville: Summer 1915," in *Death in the Family* (New York: McDowell, Obolensky, Inc., 1957), 7–8.

Paul Hammer, "The Background Word," in *Word Among Us: A Worship-centered, Lectionary-based Curriculum for the Whole Congregation* Leader's Guides (Cleveland: United Church Press, 1995), Proper 27. Used by permission.

Proper 28 (Pentecost 24)

"Done Made My Vow," traditional spiritual.

Rosemary Crumlin, *Images of Religion in Australian Art* (Kensington, New South Wales: Bay Books, 1988), 100.

Leonard Bernstein, *Mass: A Theatre Piece for Singers, Players and Dancers*, libretto by L. Bernstein and S. Schwarz (New York: Amberson Enterprises, 1971), 20.

Georg Neumark, "If Thou But Suffer God to Guide Thee," trans. Catherine Winkworth, in *The Presbyterian Hymnal* (Louisville: Westminster/John Knox, 1992), 282. Used by permission.

Fred B. Craddock et al., *Preaching Through the Christian Year: Year C* (Valley Forge, Pa.: Trinity Press International, 1994), 474.

Proper 29 (Reign of Christ)

Carter Heyward, *Touching Our Strength* (San Francisco: Harper & Row, 1989), 31–32. Used by permission of HarperCollins Publishers, Inc.

Paul Hammer, "The Background Word," in *Word Among Us: A Worship-centered, Lectionary-based Curriculum for the Whole Congregation* Leader's Guides (Cleveland: United Church Press, 1995), Proper 29. Used by permission.

Rainer Maria Rilke, "For the Sake of a Single Poem," from *The Notebooks of Malte Laurids Brigge* (New York: Random House, 1983), 91.

"Prayer of Confession," from the Sunday service of worship, International Fellowship of Metropolitan Community Church, Key West, Florida. Used by permission.

Advent 1

Philipp Nicolai, " 'Sleepers, Wake!' A Voice Astounds Us," trans. Carl P. Daw, Jr., and others, *Rejoice in the Lord: A Hymn Companion to the Scriptures*, ed. Erik Routley (Grand Rapids: Eerdmans,1985).

Alberto Taulè, "Toda la Tierra (All Earth Is Waiting)," trans. Gertrude C. Suppe, in *The New Century Hymnal* (Cleveland: Pilgrim Press, 1995). Words Copyright © 1972 The Pastoral Musicians. English translation Copyright © 1989 The United Methodist Publishing House. Used by permission.

Miriam Therese Winter, "Christmas Eve," in *God-with-Us: Resources for Prayer and Praise* (Philadelphia: Medical Mission Sisters, 1979), 22–23. Used by permission of the publisher, Abingdon Press.

Advent 2

Menachem Begin, on signing the Egyptian-Israeli peace treaty at Camp David.

Miriam Therese Winter, "Root of Jesse," in *God-with-Us: Resources for Prayer and Praise* (Philadelphia: Medical Mission Sisters, 1979), 85. Used by permission of the publisher, Abingdon Press.

"Conclusion Number 2 to Prayer for the People," in *A New Zealand Prayer Book: He Karakia Mihinare o Aotearoa* (Auckland, New Zealand: William Collins, 1989), 464. Used by permission.

Advent 3

"Joy Shall Come," Hebrew traditional.

Pierre Teilhard de Chardin, "Blessed Are You," in *Earth Prayers from Around the World,* ed. Elizabeth Roberts and Elias Amidon (San Francisco: Harper San Francisco, 1991), 200–201. Used by permission.

E. E. Cummings, "i thank You God for most this amazing," in *Complete Poems, 1904–1962,* ed. George J. Firmage (New York: Liveright, 1991), 464. © 1950, 1978, and 1991 by the Trustees for the E. E. Cummings Trust; © 1979 by George J. Firmage. Used by permission of the publisher, Liveright Publishing Corp.

"The Desert Will Sing and Rejoice," in *Iona Community Worship Book* (Glasgow, Scotland: Wild Goose Publications, 1991). Used by permission.

Advent 4

Alberto Taulè, "Toda la Tierra (All Earth Is Waiting)," trans. Gertrude C. Suppe, in *The New Century Hymnal* (Cleveland: Pilgrim Press, 1995). Words Copyright © 1972 The Pastoral Musicians. English translation Copyright © 1989 The United Methodist Publishing House. Used by permission.

Wayne Saffen, *The First Season, Advent, Christmas, Epiphany* (Philadelphia: Fortress Press, 1973), 54–55. Used by permission of Augsburg Fortress Publishers.

Allan Boesak, adapted from an address for the World Council of Churches, in *Bread of Tomorrow: Prayers for the Church Year,* ed. Janet Morley (Maryknoll, N.Y.: Orbis Books; London, Christian Aid, 1992), 31. Used by permission.

Christmas

John Rutter, "Candlelight Carol" (London: Oxford University Press, 1985). Used by permission of Hinshaw Music, Inc.

Geoffrey Ainger, "Born in the Night, Mary's Child," in *The Presbyterian Hymnal* (Louisville: Westminster/John Knox, 1990), 30. Words © Stainer & Bell, Ltd. All rights reserved. Used by permission of Hope Publishing Co.

"Collect for the First Sunday After Christmas," in *A New Zealand Prayer Book: He Karakia Mihinare o Aotearoa* (Auckland, New Zealand: William Collins Publishers, 1989), 557. Used by permission.

John 1:3–5, from *An Inclusive-Language Lectionary: Readings for Year A,* rev. ed. (New York: Pilgrim Press, 1986). Used by permission.

Christmas 1

Alberto Taulè, "Toda la Tierra (All Earth Is Waiting)," trans. Gertrude C. Suppe, in *The New Century Hymnal* (Cleveland: Pilgrim Press, 1995). Words Copyright © 1972 The Pastoral Musicians. English translation Copyright © 1989 The United Methodist Publishing House. Used by permission.

Christmas 2

Madeleine L'Engle, *The Irrational Season* (New York: Seabury Press, 1977), 18.

Bernard of Clairvaux, in *The HarperCollins Book of Prayers: A Treasury of Prayers through the Ages,* compiled by Robert Van de Weyer (San Francisco: HarperSan Francisco, 1993), 64.

Susan Virginia Hull, *United Church of Christ Sunday Bulletin Service,* December 12, 1993.

Fred B. Craddock et al., *Preaching Through the Christian Year: A* (Philadelphia: Trinity Press International, 1992).

Julia Esquivel, "Those Who Saw the Star," in *Threatened with Resurrection* (Elgin, Ill.: Brethren Press, 1982), 31–33. Used by permission.

Epiphany

Raymond E. Brown, *The Birth of the Messiah: A Commentary of the Infancy Narratives in Matthew and Luke* (New York: Doubleday, 1977), 199.

T. S. Eliot, "Journey of the Magi," in *Collected Poems 1909–1962* (New York: Harcourt Brace Jovanovich, 1964), 97–98. © 1964 by T. S. Eliot. Used by permission of Harcourt Brace & Co.

Gian Carlo Menotti, *Amahl and the Night Visitors* (New York: Whittlesey House, 1952). Used by permission.

Miriam Therese Winter, "Light of the World," in *Womanpower, Womansong: Resources for Ritual* (Philadelphia: Medical Mission Sisters, 1987), 83. Used by permission of Crossroad Publishers.

Epiphany 1

Anonymous, "Beatitudes for Friends and Family," in *That All May Worship: An Interfaith Welcome to People with Disabilities* (Washington, D.C.: National Organization on Disability, 1992), 39. Used by permission.

Fred D. Gealy, "Cornelius," in *The Interpreter's Dictionary of the Bible,* ed. George Arthur Buttrick (Nashville: Abingdon Press, 1962), 699. Used by permission.

Toc H., "Almighty God, as your Son our Saviour was born of a Hebrew mother," in *The Oxford Book of Prayer* (London: Oxford University Press, 1985), no. 218.

Rick Yramategui, "Hear Our Voices," Iowa City, Iowa. Used by permission.

Epiphany 2

William Blake, "The Lamb," in *Poetry and Prose of William Blake* (New York: Doubleday, 1965), 8–9.

Denise Levertov, "Mass for the Day of St. Thomas Didymus" (excerpt), in *Candles in Babylon* (New York: New Directions, 1982). Used by permission.

"Agnus Dei," early Christian hymn.

Epiphany 3

Franta Bass, "I Am a Jew," in *I Never Saw Another Butterfly: Children's Drawings and Poems from Terezin Concentration Camp*, ed. Hana Volavkova (New York: Schocken Books, 1993), 57. Used by permission of the U.S. Holocaust Memorial Society and the Prague State Jewish Museum.

William Dean Clark, unpublished letter. Used by permission of Anderson Clark.

Philip Andrews, "The Song of the Magi," in *Suffering and Hope*, ed. Ron O'Grady and Lee Soo Jin (Singapore: Christian Conference of Asia, 1976). Used by permission of Pace Publishing Co.

Epiphany 4

Walter Brueggemann, "Voices of the Night: Against Justice," in *To Act Justly, Love Tenderly, Walk Humbly: An Agenda for Ministers*, ed. Walter Brueggemann, Sharon Parks, and Thomas Groome (Mahwah, N.J.: Paulist Press, 1986), 7.

Jane Parker Huber, "Called as Partners in Christ's Service," words Copyright © 1981 Jane Parker Huber. From *A Singing Faith*. Used by permission of Westminster/John Knox Press.

Henri Nouwen, "Foreword," in Gustavo Gutiérrez, *We Drink from Our Own Wells* (Maryknoll, N.Y.: Orbis, 1984), xiv–xv. Used by permission.

Epiphany 5

Stephen Schwartz, excerpt from "You Are the Light of the World," from *Godspell* (New York: Harold Square Music Co. and Cadenza Music Corp., 1971). © 1971 Range Road Music, Inc., Quartet Music, Inc., and New Cadenza Music Corp. All rights reserved. Used by permission.

Benjamin F. Chavis, Jr., *Psalms from Prison* (Cleveland: Pilgrim Press, 1994), 140. Used by permission.

"This Little Light of Mine," traditional African American spiritual.

Jim Cotter, "Give to Each of Us a Candle of the Spirit," in *With All God's People: The New Ecumenical Prayer Cycle* (Geneva: WCC Publications, 1989).

John P. Meier, *Matthew* (Wilmington, Del.: Michael Glazier, 1980).

Proper 1 (Epiphany 6)

Mechthild of Magdeburg, "True Sorrow," in *The Soul Afire: Revelations of the Mystics*, ed. H. A. Reinhold (New York: Pantheon, 1944), 113.

Julian of Norwich, *Meditations with Julian of Norwich*, ed. Brendon Doyle (Santa Fe: Bear and Co., 1983). Used by permission.

Jeremiah Ingalls, "The Garden Hymn," in *The Sacred Harp*, 1859.

Carl Holladay, "1 Corinthians 3:1–9," in Fred B. Craddock et al., *Preaching through the Christian Year: A* (Philadelphia: Trinity Press International, 1992), 113.

Transfiguration Sunday

John Aurelio, *Myth Man: A Storyteller's Jesus* (New York: Crossroad, 1993), 118, 119. Used by permission.

Wolfgang Amadeus Mozart, *The Magic Flute* (Bryn Mawr, Pa.: O. Ditson, 1888).

Flannery O'Connor, "The Peeler," in *The Complete Stories of Flannery O'Connor* (New York: Farrar, Straus & Giroux, 1979), 72. Copyright © 1949 by Flannery O'Connor. Copyright © renewed 1977 by the Estate of Mary Flannery O'Connor. Used by permission of Farrar, Straus & Giroux, Inc.

Thomas H. Troeger, "Swiftly Pass the Clouds of Glory," in *The Presbyterian Hymnal* (Louisville: Westminster/John Knox, 1990), 73. Used by permission.

Ash Wednesday

Rudolfo Anaya, *Bless Me, Ultima* (Berkeley, Calif.: TQS Publications, 1972), 195.

"The Invitation and Prayer Before the Imposition of Ashes," *The Book of Alternative Services of the Anglican Church of Canada* (General Synod of the Anglican Church of Canada, 1985), 59. Used by permission.

Annie Dillard, *An American Childhood* (New York: Harper & Row, 1987), 25. Used by permission of HarperCollins Publishers, Inc.

Ursula K. LeGuin, "We Are Dust," in *Hard Words and Other Poems* (New York: Harper & Row, 1981), 70. Used by permission of HarperCollins Publishers, Inc.

Lent 1

Mary Shelley, *Frankenstein or the Modern Prometheus* (New York: New American Library, 1978), xi.

"Because the World Is a Beautiful Thing" (excerpt), in *The Iona Community Worship Book* (Glasgow, Scotland: Iona Community/Wild Goose Worship Group, 1988), 47. Used by permission.

Richard Bach, *One* (New York: Dell, 1988), 121.

Sara M. deHall, "Si Fui Motivo de Dolor, Oh Dios (If I Have Been the Source of Pain, O God)," based on text by C. M. Battersby, trans. Janet W. May, in *The New Century Hymnal* (Cleveland, Pilgrim Press, 1995). English translation Copyright ©1992 United Church Board for Homeland Ministries/Pilgrim Press, Cleveland, Ohio. Used by permission.

Carl Gustav Jung, *The New Book of Christian Quotations* (New York: Crossroad, 1983), 226.

Lent 2

Stuart Hample and Eric Marshall, *Children's Letters to God: The New Collection* (New York: Workman, 1991), 34. Used by permission.

Sojourner Truth, *Narrative of Sojourner Truth* (New York: Arno Press, 1878; New York Times, 1969), 67.

Pearl S. Buck, *The Big Wave* (New York: John Day, 1947), 48–49.

Rubem A. Alves, "My God, I need to have signs of your grace," in *Bread of Tomorrow: Prayers for the Church Year*, ed. Janet Morley (Maryknoll, N.Y.: Orbis Books; London: Christian Aid, 1992), 71.

Lent 3

Miriam Therese Winter, "A Psalm on Living Water," *Woman Word* (Hartford, Conn.: Crossroad, 1990), 111. © 1990 Medical Mission Sisters. Used by permission of the Crossroad Publishing Co., New York.

Esther de Waal, "In the Name of God," in *Every Earthly Blessing* (Ann Arbor: Servant Publications, 1991), 29–30. Used by permission.

Wang Weifen, "My Lord Is the Source of Love," in *Lilies of the Field*, trans. Janet and Philip Wickeri, Foundation for Theological Studies in Southeast Asia, 1988, quoted in *Bread of Tomorrow: Prayers for the Church Year*, ed. Janet Morley (Maryknoll, N.Y.: Orbis Books; 1992), 136. Used by permission.

Raymond E. Brown, *The Gospel According to John I–XII* (Garden City, N.Y.: Doubleday, 1966), 178.

Lent 4

Robert A. Spivey and D. Moody Smith, *Anatomy of the New Testament: A Guide to Its Structure and Meaning* (New York: Macmillan, 1982), 220.

Helen Keller, *The Story of My Life* (New York: Doubleday, Page and Co., 1903), 23–24.

Shusaku Endo, *Silence* (New York: Taplinger, 1980), 258.

Lent 5

Christopher R. Seitz, "Expository Article on Ezekiel 37:1–14," *Interpretation: A Journal of Bible and Theology* 46 (1992): 55.

Toni Morrison, *Beloved* (New York: Plume, 1987), 87–89. Used by permission.

Kate Compston, excerpt from "Litany of the Four Elements," in *Bread of Tomorrow: Prayers for the Church Year*, ed. Janet Morley (Maryknoll, N.Y.: Orbis Books; London: Christian Aid, 1992), 157.

"Zuni Chant," in *Earth Prayers from Around the World*, ed. Elizabeth Roberts and Elias Amidon (San Francisco: Harper San Francisco, 1991), 161. Used by permission of Sierra Club Books.

Palm/Passion Sunday

Natalie Sleeth, "Little Grey Donkey" (Dallas: Choristers Guild, 1970). Used by permission.

Rubén Ruiz, "Hosanna," trans. Gertrude C. Suppe, in *Supplement to the Book of Hymns of the United Methodist Church* (Nashville: Abingdon). Used by permission.

"The Covenant of Peace: A Liberation Prayer," in *The Wideness of God's Mercy: Litanies to Enlarge Our Prayer*, ed. Jeffery W. Rowthorn (Minneapolis: Seabury, 1985), 1:103–4. Used by permission of John Pairman Brown.

Madeleine L'Engle, *The Glorious Impossible* (New York: Simon & Schuster, 1990), 27.

Holy Thursday

Michael E. Moynahan, "Friends Meeting," in Eileen Elizabeth Freeman, *The Holy Week Book* (San Jose, Calif.: Resource Publications, 1979), 43. Copyright © 1979 by Resource Publications, Inc., 160 E. Virginia Street #290, San Jose, CA 95112. Used by permission.

"Jesu, Jesu," Ghana folk song adapted by Tom Colvin (Carol Stream, Ill.: Hope Publishing Co., 1969). Used by permission.

Good Friday

A Book of Worship for Free Churches (New York: Oxford University Press, 1950), 71.

Anderson Clark, unpublished letter. Used by permission.

Kathleen T. Talvacchia, "Contradictions of the Cross," in *C & C*, February 17, 1992, 28–29.

Martin Luther King, Jr., "The Cross We Bear," speech given January 12, 1963, at the National Conference on Religion and Race, Chicago, Illinois. Reprinted by arrangement with the heirs to the Estate of Martin Luther King, Jr., c/o Joan Daves Agency as agent for the proprietor. Copyright 1963 by Martin Luther King, Jr.; copyright renewed 1991 by Coretta Scott King.

Easter

Paul Hammer, "The Background Word," in *Word Among Us: A Worship-centered, Lectionary-based Curriculum for the Whole Congregation* Leader's Guides (Cleveland: United Church Press, 1995), Easter. Used by permission.

Countee Cullen, "The Black Christ," from *My Soul's High Song: The Collected Writings of Countee Cullen, Voice of the Harlem Renaissance*, ed. Gerald Early (New York: Doubleday, 1991) 232–233. Used by permission of the Cullen Estate.

Jane Dillenberger, *Image and Spirit in Sacred and Secular Art* (New York: Crossroad, 1990), 130–31.

"Easter Sequence," from "Easter Sunday Mass," translation from the Latin in Elizabeth A. Johnson, *She Who Is: The Mystery of God in Feminist Theological Discourse* (New York: Crossroad, 1993), 160. Used by permission.

Easter 2

Thomas H. Troeger, "These Things Did Thomas Count," words Copyright © 1984 Oxford University Press. Used by permission.

Kahlil Gibran, *New Oxford Book of Christian Quotations*, ed. Tony Castles (New York: Oxford University Press, 1986), 65.

Heather Murray Elkins, "The Younger Brother of Thomas," *Accent on Youth*, vol. 7, no. 2 (Spring 1985): 2. Used by permission.

Paul Tillich, *The Dynamics of Faith* (New York: Harper & Row, 1957), 22. Copyright © 1957 by Paul Tillich, and © 1985 by Hanna Tillich. Used by permission of HarperCollins Publishers, Inc.

Gustavio Gutiérrez, *We Drink from Our Own Wells* (Maryknoll, N.Y.: Orbis, 1984), 19. Used by permission.

Easter 3

Gunella Norris, "Plenty," in *Becoming Bread: Meditations on Loving and Transformation* (New York: Bell Tower, 1993), 72. Used by permission of Bell Tower Books, a division of Crown Publishers, Inc.

Gustavio Gutiérrez, *We Drink from Our Own Wells* (Maryknoll, N.Y.: Orbis, 1984), 52. Used by permission.

United Church of Christ Book of Worship (New York: United Church of Christ Office for Church Life and Leadership, 1986), 81. Used by permission.

Easter 4

Marion Soards, Thomas Dozeman, and Kendall McCabe, *Year A, Lent/Easter: Preaching the Revised Common Lectionary* (Nashville: Abingdon, 1993), 136.

Annie Dillard, *An American Childhood* (New York: Harper & Row, 1987), 198–99. Used by permission of HarperCollins Publishers, Inc.

Hazel Barkham, "House Warming," in *Daring to Speak Love's Name: A Gay and Lesbian Prayer Book*, ed. Elizabeth Stuart (London: Hamish Hamilton, 1992), 74–75.

Easter 5

Langston Hughes, "My People," in *Selected Poems* (New York: Alfred A. Knopf, 1926), 57. Used by permission.

Marilyn Robinson, "The First and Second Epistles General of Peter," in *Incarnation: Contemporary Writers on the New Testament*, ed. by Alfred Corn (New York: Penguin, 1990), 311.

United Church of Christ Book of Worship (New York: United Church of Christ Office for Church Life and Leadership, 1986), 266–67. Used by permission.

Carlo Carretto, *The God Who Comes* (London: Darton, Longman and Todd, 1981).

Easter 6

Rabindranath Tagore, in *The Bible Through Asian Eyes*, ed. Masao Takenaka and Ron O'Grady (Auckland, New Zealand: Pace Publishing in association with the Asian Christian Art Association, 1991), 165. Used by permission.

Martin B. Copenhaver, *To Begin at the Beginning: An Introduction to the Christian Faith* (Cleveland: United Church Press, 1994), 57. Used by permission.

Jean Vanier, *The Broken Body: Journey to Wholeness* (New York: Paulist Press, 1988), 69.

Easter 7

Stephen Spender, in *The Oxford Book of English Verse*, ed. Helen Gardner (New York: Oxford University Press, 1972), 929–30. Used by permission of Faber & Faber.

"Night Prayer" (excerpt), in *A New Zealand Prayer Book: He Karakia Mihinare o Aotearoa* (Auckland, New Zealand: William Collins Publishers, Ltd., 1989), 184. Used by permission.

St. Francis of Assisi, in *The Oxford Book of Prayer*, ed. George Appleton (New York: Oxford University Press, 1985), 63.

Pentecost Sunday

Christina Rossetti, *The Complete Poems of Christina Rossetti*, vol. 2 (Baton Rouge: Louisiana State University Press, 1979).

"Veni Sancte Spiritus," words—Come Holy Spirit; verses drawn from the *Pentecost Sequence*, Taizé Community, 1978. Music: Jacques Berthier, Copyright ©1979 Les Presses de Taize (France). Used by permission of G.I.A. Publications, Inc., Chicago, Illinois, exclusive agent. All rights reserved.

Jan Berry, "Exuberant Spirit of God," in *Bread of Tomorrow: Prayers for the Church Year*, ed. Janet Morley (Maryknoll, N.Y.: Orbis Books; London: Christian Aid, 1992), 129. Used by permission.

Trinity Sunday (Pentecost 1)

"An African Canticle," in *Earth Prayers from Around the World*, ed. Elizabeth Roberts and Elias Amidon (San Francisco: Harper San Francisco, 1991), 219. Used by permission of The Church Missionary Society.

St. Catherine of Siena, "Prayer 11, lines 105–112," in *The Prayers of Catherine of Siena*, ed. Suzanne Noffke (New York: Paulist Press, 1983), 89. Used by permission.

Ernesto Cardenal, "Bless the Lord, O My Soul," in *Earth Prayers from Around the World*, ed. Elizabeth Roberts and Elias Amidon (San Francisco: Harper San Francisco, 1991), 224.

Carmelites of Indianapolis, "Glory to You," in *The New Companion to the Breviary with Seasonal Supplement* (Indianapolis: Carmelites of Indianapolis, 1988), 1. Used by permission.

Proper 5 (Pentecost 2)

Walter Brueggemann, *Genesis, Interpretation: A Bible Commentary for Teaching and Preaching* (Atlanta: John Knox Press, 1982).

Jeffrey W. Rowthorn, *The Wideness of God's Mercy: Litanies to Enlarge Our Prayer* (Minneapolis: The Seabury Press, 1985), 1:47.

"Prayer Number 3," in *A New Zealand Prayer Book: He Karakia Mihinare o Aotearoa* (Auckland, New Zealand: William Collins Publishers, Ltd., 1989), 465. Used by permission.

Robert Allen Warrior, "Canaanites, Cowboys and Indians," in *Ethics in the Present Tense: Readings from Christianity and Crisis, 1966–1991*, ed. Leon Howell and Vivian Lindermayer (New York: Friendship Press, 1991), 50.

"Prayer for Wednesday Evening," in *A New Zealand Prayer Book: He Karakia Mihinare o Aotearoa* (Auckland, New Zealand: William Collins Publishers, Ltd., 1989), 123. Used by permission.

Leopold Sedar Senghor, "Part V, Prayer for Peace," in *Leopold Sedar Senghor: The Collected Poetry*, trans. Melvin Dixon (Charlottesville: University Press of Virginia, 1991), 72. Used by permission.

Proper 6 (Pentecost 3)

Judy Gattis Smith, "Sarah Laughed," Copyright © 1993. All rights reserved. Used by permission.

Chana Bloch, "Magnificat," in *Secrets of the Tribe* (Riverdale-on-Hudson, N.Y.: Sheep Meadow Press, 1981), 65–66. Used by permission.

Isak Dinesan, *Winter's Tale* (New York: Random House, 1942), 122.

Frederick Buechner, *Peculiar Treasures: A Biblical Who's Who* (San Francisco: Harper & Row, 1979), 153. Used by permission of HarperCollins Publishers, Inc.

Teresa of Avila, "Silly Devotions," in *Famous Prayers*, compiled by Veronica Zundel (Grand Rapids, Mich.: Eerdmans, 1983), 51.

Proper 7 (Pentecost 4)

Symeon the New Theologian, "We Awaken in Christ's Body," trans. and adapted by Stephen Mitchell, in *The Enlightened Heart: An Anthology of Sacred Poetry* (New York: Harper & Row, 1989), 38. Used by permission.

William H. Willimon, *Remember Who You Are: Baptism, A Model for Christian Life* (Nashville: The Upper Room, 1980), 103.

Julia Esquivel, "I Am No Longer Afraid of Death," in *Threatened with Resurrection* (Elgin, Ill.: Brethren Press, 1982), 66–67. Used by permission.

Proper 8 (Pentecost 5)

Monika Hellwig, *The Eucharist and the Hunger of the World* (New York: Paulist Press, 1976). Used by permission.

An Old Gaelic Rune (Dublin: The Cuala Press).

Kathleen Norris, *Dakota: A Spiritual Geography* (New York: Houghton Mifflin, 1993), 191.

Linda Hogan, "What Holds the Water, What Holds the Light," in *Parabola: Magazine of Myth and Tradition*, vol. 12, no. 1 (Winter 1990): 14.

Proper 9 (Pentecost 6)

John P. Meier, *Matthew* (Wilmington, Del.: Michael Glazier, 1980), 148.

Susan Cady, Marian Ronan, and Hal Taussig, *Wisdom's Feast* (New York: Harper & Row, 1989), 154–55, adapted for inclusivity. Used by permission.

Henry Richard McFadyen, "The Lone, Wild Bird," in *The Presbyterian Hymnal* (Louisville: Westminster/John Knox, 1990). Used by permission of Catholic Polls, Inc.

Traditional English child's evening prayer.

Proper 10 (Pentecost 7)

April Oursler Armstrong, *The Tales Christ Told,* adapted from Fulton Oursler, *The Greatest Story Ever Told: The Life of Christ* (New York: Doubleday, 1958), 9, 17, 18.

Katie Breeze, *Nekkid Cowboy* (San Antonio: Corona Publishing, 1991), 54–55. Used by permission.

Paul Hammer, "The Background Word," in *Word Among Us: A Worship-centered, Lectionary-based Curriculum for the Whole Congregation* Leader's Guides (Cleveland: United Church Press, 1995), Proper 10. Used by permission.

Charles Singer and Albert Hari, *Experience Jesus Today* (Strasbourg, France: Éditions du Signe, 1993), 99. Distributed by Oregon Catholic Press. Used by permission.

Proper 11 (Pentecost 8)

John Milton, *Paradise Lost,* Book x, 177, in *The Portable Milton,* ed. Douglas Bush (New York: Viking, 1949), 475.

Flannery O'Connor, "The Artificial Nigger," in *Flannery O'Connor: The Complete Stories* (New York: Farrar, Straus & Giroux, 1979), 269–70. Used by permission of Harcourt Brace & Co.

"A Midday Prayer" (excerpt), in *A New Zealand Prayer Book: He Karakia Mihinare o Aotearoa* (Auckland: William Collins, Ltd., 1989), 162. Used by permission.

John P. Meier, *Matthew* (Wilmington, Del.: Michael Glazier, 1980), 18.

Proper 12 (Pentecost 9)

Gunilla Norris, "The Second Rising," in *Becoming Bread: Meditations on Loving and Transformation* (New York: Bell Tower, 1993), 56. Used by permission of Bell Tower Books, a division of Crown Publishers, Inc.

Thomas McGrath, "Bread of This World; Praises III," in *Selected Poems: 1938–1988* (Port Townsend, Wash.: Copper Canyon Press, 1988). Used by permission.

Seamus Heaney, "Field of Vision," in *Seeing Things* (New York: Farrar, Straus & Giroux, 1991), 24. Copyright © 1991 by Seamus Heaney. Used by permission of Farrar, Straus & Giroux, Inc.

T. S. Eliot, excerpt from "Little Gidding," in *Four Quartets* (New York: Harcourt Brace Jovanovich, 1943), 39. Copyright 1943 by T. S. Eliot and renewed in 1971 by Esme Valerie Eliot. Used by permission of Harcourt Brace & Co.

William Shakespeare, *Henry VI, Part 2,* act iii, scene 3.1, in *The Complete Works of William Shakespeare,* ed. W. G. Clark and W. Aldis Wright (Garden City, N.Y.: Doubleday, n.d.), 166.

Proper 13 (Pentecost 10)

Charles Wesley, "Wrestling Jacob," in *The Penguin Book of English Christian Verse,* ed. Peter Levi (London: Penguin, 1984), 176–77.

Elie Wiesel, *Messengers of God: Biblical Portraits and Legends* (New York: Random House, 1976), 94.

Linda Clark, "A Sermon: Wrestling with Jacob's Angel," in Linda Clark, Marian Ronan, and Eleanor Walker, *Image-Breaking, Image Building* (New York: Pilgrim Press, 1981), 101. Used by permission.

Tony Kushner, *Angels in America, Part One: Millenium Approaches* (New York: Theatre Communications Group, 1993), 49-50. Used by permission.

Carter Heyward, *Staying Power: Reflections on Faith, Gender, and Justice* (Cleveland: Pilgrim Press, 1995).

Proper 14 (Pentecost 11)

Sören Kierkegaard, *Concluding Unscientific Postscript,* ed. and trans. Howard B. Hong and Edna H. Hong (Princeton, N.J.: Princeton University Press, 1992), 288, 470–71, 477. Used by permission.

Martin Luther, adapted from Prayer #18 in *Luther's Prayers,* ed. Herbert F. Brokering (Minneapolis: Augsburg, 1967), 8.

May Sarton, *Journal of a Solitude* (New York: Norton, 1973), 58.

Gabrielle Hadingham, "Prayer #268," in *Oxford Book of Prayer,* ed. George Appleton (New York: Oxford Univeristy Press, 1985), 89. Used by permission of SLG Press.

Douglas R. A. Hare, *Matthew: Interpretation, A Bible Commentary for Teaching and Preaching* (Louisville: John Knox, 1993), 169.

Proper 15 (Pentecost 12)

Jacob Lawrence, *Toussaint L'Ouverture Series Catalogue,* ed. James Buell (New York: The United Church Board for Homeland Ministries, 1982), 21. Used by permission.

Dietrich Bonhoeffer, *The Cost of Discipleship* (New York: Macmillan, 1963).

Anonymous prayer.

"Hine Ma Tov (How Very Good and Pleasant It Is)," Hebrew traditional, arrangement copyright © 1994 by United Church Press. Used by permission.

Proper 16 (Pentecost 13)

Henri Nouwen, *The Road to Daybreak: A Spiritual Journey* (New York: Doubleday, 1988), 150–51. Used by permission of Doubleday, a division of Bantam Doubleday Dell Publishing Group, Inc.

Virginia Mollenkott, *Godding: Human Responsibility and the Bible* (New York: Crossroad, 1987), 39. Used by permission.

Clarice Martin, "The Background Word," in *Word Among Us: A Worship-centered, Lectionary-based Curriculum for the Whole Congregation* Leader's Guides (Cleveland: United Church Press, 1995), Proper 16. Used by permission.

Al Carmines, *Many Gifts, One Spirit,* unpublished writings, New York, New York. Used by permission.

Illustration Sources

Foreword

Manuel Alvarez Bravo, *The Public Fountain*, 1934, Victoria and Albert Museum, London, England (Art Resource, N.Y.). Used by permission.

Praying and Imaging: The Art of Contemplation

Bagong Kussudiardja, *The Ascension*, in *The Bible Through Asian Eyes*, ed. Masao Takenaka and Ron O'Grady (Auckland, New Zealand: Pace Publishing in association with the Asian Christian Art Association, 1991), 165. Used by permission.

Jonathan Green, *Tales*, 1988, oil on masonite, Jonathan Green Studios, Inc., Naples, Florida. Used by permission.

Noel Counihan, *Homage to Goya (Requiem for El Salvador)*, 1985, collection of Pat Counihan, Melbourne, Australia. Used by permission.

Francisco Goya, *Third of May, 1808*, Prado, Madrid, Spain (Scala/Art Resource, N.Y.). Used by permission.

Graham Sutherland, *The Crucifixion*, 1946, St. Matthew's Church, Northampton, England. Used by permission of the Vicar of St. Matthew's Church, Northampton, England.

Ellis Wilson, *Funeral Procession*, The Amistad Research Center, New Orleans, Louisiana. Used by permission.

God's Big World—An Adventure for Children

Carmen Lomas Garza, *Camas para Sueños (Beds for Dreams)*, San Francisco, California. Used by permission.

Giotto, *Entry into Jerusalem*, c. 1305, Scrovegni Chapel, Padua, Italy (Scala/ Art Resource, N.Y.). Used by permission.

Rembrandt Harmensz van Rijn, *Two Women Teaching a Child to Walk*, c. 1640, © The British Museum, London, England. Used by permission.

Adolph Gottlieb, *Apaquogue*, 1961, oil on canvas, The Benjamin J. Tillar Memorial Trust, collection of the Modern Art Museum of Fort Worth. Used by permission.

Seasonal Divider for Pentecost (Cycle B)

Jonathan Green, *Tales*, detail, 1988, oil on masonite, Jonathan Green Studios, Inc., Naples, Florida. Used by permission.

Proper 17 (Pentecost 13)

Jack Baron, *The Picnic*, 1989, Key West, Florida. Used by permission.

Kathryn Abbe, *Tea Party*, Glen Head, New York. Used by permission.

Edward Hopper, *Nighthawks*, 1942, oil on canvas, Friends of American Art Collection, 1942.51, Art Institute of Chicago. Photograph © 1994. All rights reserved. Used by permission.

Proper 18 (Pentecost 14)

Jacob Lawrence, *And God created man and woman, Genesis Series VII*, Francine Seders Gallery, Ltd., Seattle, Washington. Used by permission.

Carmen Lomas Garza, *Camas para Sueños (Beds for Dreams)*, San Francisco, California. Used by permission.

Meinrad Craighead, *Changing Woman*, 1982, ink on scratchboard, as reproduced in *The Mother's Songs* (Mahwah, N.J.: Paulist Press, 1986), 32. Collection of Myrna Little, Texas. © Meinrad Craighead. Used by permission.

Proper 19 (Pentecost 15)

Jean Édouard Vuillard, *Woman Sweeping*, 1899–1900, Phillips Collection, Washington, D.C. Used by permission.

Bud Lee, *Reverend Howard Finster's "Paradise Garden" in Summerville, Georgia*, as reproduced in C. Kurt Dewhurst, Betty MacDowell, and Marsha MacDowell, *Religious Folk Art in America: Reflections of Faith* (New York: E. P. Dutton, 1983), p. 108, plate 133. Used by permission of Finster Folk Art.

Proper 20 (Pentecost 16)

Pablo Picasso, *Guernica*, 1937, Centro de Arte Reine Sofia, National Museum, Madrid, Spain (Giraudon/Art Resource, N.Y.). Used by permission.

Rembrandt Harmensz van Rijn, *Jeremiah Lamenting the Destruction of Jerusalem*, 1630, Rijksmuseum, Amsterdam, The Netherlands.

Proper 21 (Pentecost 17)

Albrecht Dürer, *Knight, Death, and the Devil*, 1513, Musee du Petit Palais, Paris (Giraudon/Art Resource, N.Y.). Used by permission.

Eric Miller, *South African Demonstration*, Impact Visuals, New York, New York. © 1992. Used by permission.

Proper 22 (Pentecost 18)

Archibald John Motley, Jr., *Mending Socks*, 1924, oil on canvas, 58.1.2801, Burton Emmett Collection, Ackland Art Museum, University of North Carolina at Chapel Hill. Used by permission.

Rick Reinhard, *Laying on of Hands*, Washington, D.C. © Rick Reinhard. Used by permission.

Proper 23 (Pentecost 19)

Linda Lomahaftewa, *New Mexico Sunset*, The Heard Museum, Phoenix, Arizona. Used by permission.

Michael Kabotie, *Petroglyphs*, The Heard Museum, Phoenix, Arizona. Used by permission.

Proper 24 (Pentecost 20)

Wilmer Jennings, *De Good Book Says,* The Amistad Research Center, New Orleans, Louisiana. Used by permission.

Marc Chagall, *Moses Receiving the Tablets from the Lord,* 1950–52, collection of the artist, St. Paul de Vence, France (Giraudon/Art Resource, N.Y.). Used by permission.

Manuscript illumination, *The Beginning of the Gospel of St. John,* from the *Book of Lindesfarne,* Cotton Nero D. iv, f. 211, The British Library, London, England. Used by permission.

Proper 25 (Pentecost 21)

John Pitman Weber, *Yell,* 1990, Oak Park, Illinois. Used by permission.

Adolph Gottlieb, *Apaquogue,* 1961, oil on canvas, Benjamin J. Tillar Memorial Trust, collection of the Modern Art Museum of Fort Worth, Fort Worth, Texas. Used by permission.

All Saints' Day

Jan van Eyck, *Adoration of the Mystic Lamb, The Ghent Altarpiece,* 1432, Vijd Chapel, Cathedral St. Bravo, Ghent, Belgium (Scala/Art Resource, N.Y.). Used by permission.

Cappella della Velatio: Lunette with Orante, Catacomb of Priscilla, Rome, Italy (Scala/Art Resource, N.Y.). Used by permission.

Proper 26 (Pentecost 22)

Emil Nolde, *Hermit in a Tree,* 1931, Stiftung Seebüll Ada und Emil Nolde, Neukirchen, Germany. Used by permission.

Jonathan Green, *Tales,* 1988, oil on masonite, Jonathan Green Studios, Inc., Naples, Florida. Used by permission.

Proper 27 (Pentecost 23)

Walter Williams, *Caged Bird,* The Amistad Research Center, New Orleans, Louisiana. Used by permission.

Ellis Wilson, *Funeral Procession,* The Amistad Research Center, New Orleans, Louisiana. Used by permission.

Proper 28 (Pentecost 24)

Rembrandt Harmensz van Rijn, *Two Women Teaching a Child to Walk,* c. 1640, © The British Museum, London, England. Used by permission.

Noel Counihan, *Homage to Goya (Requiem for El Salvador),* 1985, collection of Pat Counihan, Melbourne, Australia. Used by permission.

Proper 29 (Reign of Christ)

Alma Thomas, *The Eclipse,* gift of Alma W. Thomas, National Museum of American Art, Smithsonian Institution, Washington, D.C. Used by permission.

Edward "Rainbow" Larson (designer) and Verla Shilling (quilter), *Missouri Farm, Newton County,* Santa Fe, New Mexico. Used by permission.

Seasonal Divider for Advent

D. A. Siqueiros, *Peasant Mother,* detail, 1929, Museo Nacional de Arte Moderno, Mexico City, Mexico (Giraudon/Art Resource, N.Y.). Used by permission.

Advent 1

Cross of the Community, artisans of La Palma, El Salvador.

Glen Strock, *Rapture at Rio Arriba,* Dixon, New Mexico. Used by permission.

Advent 2

C. Terry Saul, *Tree of Jesse,* The Heard Museum, Phoenix, Arizona. Used by permission.

John August Swanson, *Peaceable Kingdom,* Bergsma Gallery, Grand Rapids, Michigan. Serigraph © 1994 by John August Swanson. Used by permission of the artist.

Advent 3

William James Warren, *Deserts: Dry Lake Bed,* West Light, Los Angeles, California. Used by permission.

D. A. Siqueiros, *Peasant Mother,* 1929, Museo Nacional de Arte Moderno, Mexico City, Mexico (Giraudon/Art Resource, N.Y.). Used by permission.

Mark Edward Harris, *Oakland Fire,* Los Angeles, California. © Mark Edward Harris. Used by permission.

Advent 4

William Ebbets, *Oswaldo Chin, Beekeeper, and Manuel,* Mérida, Yucatán, Mexico. Used by permission.

Aminah Brenda Lynn Robinson, *What You Gonna Name That Pretty Little Baby?* in *The Teachings: Drawn from African-American Spirituals* (Orlando: Harcourt Brace & Co., 1992). © 1992 by Aminah Brenda Lynn Robinson. Used by permission of Harcourt Brace & Co.

Seasonal Divider for Christmas

Geertgen tot Sint Jans, *The Nativity, at Night,* detail, c. 1480–85, The National Gallery, London, England. Used by permission.

Christmas/Nativity

Geertgen tot Sint Jans, *The Nativity, at Night,* c. 1480–85, The National Gallery, London, England. Used by permission.

Virgin and Child, Coptic icon, B & U International Picture Service, Amsterdam, The Netherlands. Used by permission.

Christmas 1

Mark Wyland, *Whaling Wall VI: Hawaiian Humpbacks,* Laguna Beach, California. Used by permission.

Christmas 2

Emil Nolde, *Holy Night,* Stiftung Seebüll Emil und Ada Nolde, Neukirchen, Germany. Used by permission.

Michelangelo Buonarotti, *Awakening Prisoner,* Accademia, Florence, Italy (Nimatallah/Art Resource, N.Y.). Used by permission.

Peter Paul Rubens, *Christ,* The Fogg Museum, Harvard University, Cambridge, Mass. Used by permission.

Epiphany

James (Jacques Joseph) Tissot, *Journey of the Magi*, The Minneapolis Institute of Arts, Minnesota. Used by permission.

Adoration of the Magi, tomb of Archbishop Dietrich II von Mors, 15th century, Cologne Cathedral, Cologne, Germany (Foto Marburg/Art Resource, N.Y.). Used by permission.

Epiphany 1

Elain Christensen, *Paul Remy, Camp Jabberwocky, 1985*, Vineyard Haven, Massachusetts. © Elain Christensen. Used by permission.

Baptism of Legionnaire Cornelius by St. Peter, c. late 4th century, sarcophagus of the Miraculous Source, Musee Lapidaire d'Art Chretien, Arles, France (Erich Lessing/Art Resource, N.Y.). Used by permission.

Charles Schulz, as reproduced in *The Gospel According to Peanuts* (Glasgow, Scotland: M. E. Bratcher), 114. Used by permission of United Feature Syndicate, Inc.

Epiphany 2

Ethan Hubbard, *Young Herdsman, Peru*, as reproduced in *Straight to the Heart: Children of the World* (Chelsea, Vt.: Craftsbury Common Books, 1992). Used by permission of the photographer.

Jan van Eyck, *Adoration of the Mystic Lamb*, central panel of *The Ghent Altarpiece*, 1432, Vijd Chapel, Cathedral St. Bravo, Ghent, Belgium (Scala/Art Resource, N.Y.). Used by permission.

Epiphany 3

Sailboat, archive #1773143, as reproduced in Hana Volavkova, ed., *I Never Saw Another Butterfly: Children's Drawings and Poems from Terezin Concentration Camp, 1942–1944* (New York: Pantheon, 1978), 56–57. Used by permission of the Prague State Jewish Museum and the U.S. Holocaust Memorial Museum.

David F. Johnson, *Ellie and Raymond*, New York, New York. Used by permission.

Epiphany 4

Maerten van Heemskerck, *Tobit Burying the Dead, Feeding the Poor and Visiting the Prisoners*, private collecton.

Jack Kurtz, *Soup Kitchen*, Impact Visuals, New York, New York. © 1992. Used by permission.

Epiphany 5

Kim Woong, *The Coming of the Light*, as reproduced in Masao Takenaka, ed., *Christian Art in Asia* (Tokyo: Kyo Bun Kwan in association with the Asian Christian Art Association, 1975), 148. Used by permission.

Clifford A. Ames, *Untitled*, 1976, Key West, Florida. Used by permission.

Proper 1 (Epiphany 6)

Rex Goreleigh, *Planting*, 1943, Evans-Tibbs Collection of Afro-American Art, Washington, D.C. Used by permission.

Toby Marshall, *Irises*, Photonica, New York, New York. Used by permission.

Transfiguration Sunday

The Transfiguration, Vie de Jesus Mafa, 24 rue du Marechal Joffre, 78000 Versailles, France. Used by permission.

David C. Driskell, *Movement, The Mountain*, 1980, Evans-Tibbs Collection of Afro-American Art, Washington, D.C. Used by permission.

Seasonal Divider for Lent

José Faustino Altramirano, *Blessed Is He*, detail, as reproduced in Philip and Sally Scharper, eds., *The Gospel in Art by the Peasants of Solentiname* (Maryknoll, N.Y.: Orbis Books). Used by permission of Verlagsleiter, Peter Hammer Verlag.

Ash Wednesday

Manuscript illumination, *Receiving Ashes (March: Care of the Vines, Ash Wednesday,)* from *The Hours of the Duchess of Bourgogne*, c. 1450, Musee Conde, Chantilly, France (Giraudon/Art Resource, N.Y.). Used by permission.

Sanders Nicolson, *Untitled*, Tony Stone Images, Chicago, Illinois. Used by permission.

Lent 1

Michelangelo Buonarotti, *Original Sin and Expulsion from Paradise (The Fall of Man)*, Sistine Chapel, Vatican City (Scala/Art Resource, N.Y.). Used by permission.

Boris Karloff as the Frankenstein Monster, © Universal City Studios, Inc. Courtesy of MCA Publishing Rights, a division of MCA, Inc. Photo provided by Photofest, New York. Used by permission.

Carl Mansfield, *No Swimming Allowed*, as reproduced in *The Boy: A Photographic Essay*, ed. Georges St. Martin and Ronald C. Nelson (New York: Book Adventures, 1967), 104.

Lent 2

Eero Saarinen and Associates, architects, *Kresge Chapel at MIT*. Used by permission of the MIT Museum.

John LaFarge, *Visit of Nicodemus to Christ*, gift of William T. Evans, National Museum of American Art, Smithsonian Institution, Washington D.C. Used by permission.

Lent 3

Yoichiro Miyazaki, *Underwater*, FPG International, New York, New York. Used by permission.

Jesus and the Samaritan Woman, Catacomb of via Latina, Rome, Italy (Scala/Art Resource, N.Y.). Used by permission.

Manuel Alvarez Bravo, *The Public Fountain*, 1934, Victoria and Albert Museum, London, England (Art Resource, N.Y.). Used by permission.

Lent 4

Elijah Pierce, *The Man That Was Born Blind Restored to Sight*, 1930, carved and painted wood relief, Michael and Julie Hall Collection of American Folk Art, Milwaukee Art Museum, Wisconsin. Used by permission.

Mark Rothko, *Rothko Chapel*, Houston, Texas. Used by permission.

Lent 5

Frank Day, *Mourning at Mineral Springs,* Native American Artists Resource Collection, The Heard Museum, Phoenix, Arizona. Used by permission.

Paul Vozdic, *Dancer in Motion,* Photonica, New York, New York. Used by permission

David Hiser, *Day of the Dead Celebrations,* Tony Stone Images, Chicago, Illinois. Used by permission.

Palm/Passion Sunday

Giotto, *Entry into Jerusalem,* c. 1305, Scrovegni Chapel, Padua, Italy (Scala/Art Resource, N.Y.). Used by permission.

José Faustino Altramirano, *Blessed Is He,* as reproduced in Philip and Sally Scharper, eds., *The Gospel in Art by the Peasants of Solentiname* (Maryknoll, N.Y.: Orbis Books). Used by permission of Verlagsleiter, Peter Hammer Verlag.

Holy Thursday

Annette Gandy Fortt, *The Last Supper,* as reproduced in *Liturgy* 7, no. 1 (1987).

Carmen Lomas Garza, *Tamalada (Making Tamales),* collection of Leonila Ramirez, Don Ramons Restaurant, San Francisco, California. Used by permission of the artist.

Good Friday

Graham Sutherland, *The Crucifixion,* 1946, St. Matthew's Church, Northampton, England. Used by permission of the Vicar of St. Matthew's Church, Northampton, England.

Donatello, *Lamentation Over the Dead Christ,* 1455–60, Victoria and Albert Museum, London, England (Art Resource, N.Y.). Used by permission.

Seasonal Divider for Easter

John Biggers, *The Upper Room,* detail, Artcetra, Houston, Texas. Used by permission.

Easter

John Biggers, *The Upper Room,* Artcetra, Houston, Texas. Used by permission.

Elizabeth Catlett, *Man,* courtesy of the Hampton University Museum, Hampton, Virginia. Used by permission of the artist.

Michelangelo Buonarotti, *Risen Christ,* S. Maria sopra Minerva, Rome, Italy (Scala/Art Resource, N.Y.). Used by permission.

Easter 2

Rembrandt Harmensz van Rijn, *Doubting Thomas,* 1634, Pushkin Museum of Fine Arts, Moscow, Russia (Scala/Art Resource, N.Y.). Used by permission.

Lonnie Duka, *Untitled,* Tony Stone Images, Chicago, Illinois. Used by permission.

Easter 3

Diego Rodriguez de Silva y Velazquez, *The Moorish Kitchen Maid,* National Gallery of Ireland, Dublin, Ireland (Bridgeman/Art Resource, N.Y.). Used by permission.

Michelangelo Merisi da Caravaggio, *Supper at Emmaus,* c. 1600, National Gallery of Art, London, England (Nimatallah/Art Resource, N.Y.). Used by permission.

Easter 4

Georg Gerster, *Coptic Church,* © National Geographic Society, Washington, D.C. Used by permission.

Jacob Lawrence, *The Migration of the Negro,* 1940–41, panel 54, tempera on gesso on composition board, gift of Mrs. David M. Levy, Museum of Modern Art, New York. Photograph © 1994 the Museum of Modern Art, N.Y. Used by permission.

Henry O. Tanner, *Thankful Poor,* collection of William H. and Camille O. Cosby. Used by permission.

Easter 5

Arthur Boyd, *Moses Leading the People,* 1947 (Australia, 1920–   ). Used by permission of the Bundanon Trust, New South Wales, Australia.

John August Swanson, *Festival of Lights,* acrylic painting on masonite, Bergsma Gallery, Grand Rapids, Michigan. © 1991 John August Swanson. Used by permission of the artist.

Easter 6

Emil Nolde, *Wildly Dancing Children,* Stiftung Seebüll Ada und Emil Nolde, Neukirchen, Germany. Used by permission.

Bagong Kussudiardja, *The Ascension,* as reproduced in Masao Takenaka and Ron O'Grady, *The Bible Through Asian Eyes* (Auckland, New Zealand: Pace Publishing in association with the Asian Christian Art Association, 1991), 165. Used by permission of the Asian Christian Art Association.

Easter 7

Pablo Picasso, *Woman Crying,* 1937, Prado, Madrid, Spain (Bridgeman/Art Resource, N.Y.). © ARS. Used by permission.

George Tooker, *Girl Praying,* Hartland, Vermont. Used by permission.

Seasonal Divider for Pentecost

Pentecost, from the *Rabulla Gospel,* 586, Biblioteca Medicea Laurenziana, Florence, Italy. Used by permission.

Pentecost Sunday

Oscar Howe, *Ghost Dance,* 1960, The Heard Museum, Phoenix Arizona. © 1983 by Adelheid Howe. Used by permission.

Pentecost, from the *Rabbula Gospel,* 586, Biblioteca Medicea Laurenziana, Florence, Italy. Used by permission.

Trinity Sunday (Pentecost 1)

Untitled painting as reproduced in *A Child's History of Hawaii* (Honolulu: Island Heritage, Ltd.), 30–31. Used by permission of Island Heritage and the Easter Seal Society.

Kenneth Noland, *The Gift,* 1961–62, Tate Gallery, London, England (Art Resource, N.Y.). Used by permission.

Proper 5 (Pentecost 2)

Jacopo Bassano, *Abraham's Journey*, Staatliche Museum, Berlin, Germany.

John Mix Stanley, *Oregon City on the Willamette River*, c. 1850–52, oil on canvas, Amon Carter Museum, Fort Worth, Texas. Used by permission.

Proper 6 (Pentecost 3)

Rembrandt Harmensz van Rijn, *Abraham Entertaining the Three Angels*, 1656, private collection.

Ethan Hubbard, *Margaret Ovid at Church*, as reproduced in *Faces of Wisdom: Elders of the World* (Chelsea, Vt.: Craftsbury Common Books, 1993). Used by permission.

Proper 7 (Pentecost 4)

David Alan Harvey, *Baptism*, © National Geographic Society, Washington, D.C. Used by permission.

Harriet Backer, *Baptism in Tanum Church, 1892*, Nasjonalgalleriet, Oslo, Norway. Photograph © J. Lathion. Used by permission.

Proper 8 (Pentecost 5)

John Hopper, *Rwandan Starving Children*, © AP/Wide World Photos, N.Y. Used by permission.

Andrei Rublev, *Icon of the Trinity*, c. 1411, Tretyakov Gallery, Moscow, Russia (Scala/Art Resource, N.Y.). Used by permission.

Proper 9 (Pentecost 6)

Henry Moore, *Memorial Figure, 1945–46, Horton Stone*, as reproduced in Henry Moore and John Hedgecoe, *Henry Moore: My Ideas, Inspiration and Life as an Artist* (London: Ebury Press), 195. Used by permission.

Robert Lentz, *Christ the Bridegroom*, Bridge Building Images, Burlington, Vermont. Used by permission.

Proper 10 (Pentecost 7)

Vincent van Gogh, *The Sower*, Rijksmuseum Kroeller-Mueller, Otterlo, The Netherlands (Erich Lessing/Art Resource, N.Y.). Used by permission.

Betsy James, *Double Spiral*, Albuquerque, New Mexico. Used by permission.

Vincent van Gogh, *Wheat Field with Crows*, Van Gogh Museum, Amsterdam, The Netherlands (Art Resource, N.Y.). Used by permission.

Proper 11 (Pentecost 8)

Patrick DesJarlait, *Gathering Wild Rice*, 1971, from the collection of James T. Bialac, The Heard Museum, Phoenix, Arizona. Used by permission of the Patrick DesJarlait Estate.

Soichi Sunami, *Martha Graham and Group in "Heretic,"* 1929, Dance Collection, New York Public Library for the Performing Arts, Astor, Lenox, and Tilden Foundations, New York. Used by permission of the Sunami Estate.

Proper 12 (Pentecost 9)

Jan Vermeer, *Woman Holding a Balance*, Widener Collection, National Gallery of Art, Smithsonian Institution, Washington, D.C. © 1994 by the Board of Trustees. Used by permission.

Suzanne Marshall, *Journey Through Time*, Clayton, Missouri. Photograph by RED ELF. Used by permission.

Jacopo Bassano, *The Miraculous Draught of Fishes*, Matthieson Fine Arts, London, England. Used by permission.

Proper 13 (Pentecost 10)

Martha Lewis, *Wrestlers*, New York, New York. Used by permission.

Paul Gauguin, *Vision after the Sermon (Jacob Wrestling with the Angel)*, 1888, National Gallery of Scotland, Edinburgh, Great Britain (Bridgeman/Art Resource, N.Y.). Used by permission.

Proper 14 (Pentecost 11)

Winslow Homer, *On a Lee Shore*, 1900, Museum of Art, Rhode Island School of Design, Providence, Rhode Island. Used by permission.

Henry O. Tanner, *Christ Walking on Water*, 1910, Evans-Tibbs Collection of Afro-American Art, Washington, D.C. Used by permission.

Proper 15 (Pentecost 12)

Palmer Hayden, *Midsummer Night in Harlem*, The African-American Art Museum, Los Angeles, California. Used by permission.

Ben Shahn, mosaic mural at LeMoyne-Owen College, Memphis, Tennessee. Used by permission.

Proper 16 (Pentecost 13)

Michelangelo Buonarotti, *The Study of St. Sebastian*, Louvre Museum, Paris, France (Art Resource, N.Y.). Used by permission.

Hildegard of Bingen, *All Creatures Celebrate*, illumination 15, as reproduced in Matthew Fox, *Illuminations of Hildegard of Bingen* (Santa Fe: Bear & Co., 1985). Used by permission of Bear & Co.

Index of Focus Scriptures